Santa Monica Public Library

I SMP 00 1082935 Z

P9-CRO-091

FAIRVIEW BRANCH
SANTA MONICA PUBLIC LIBRARY

OCT   1998

PIONEER DAYS

PIONEER DAYS

Discover the Past with Fun Projects, Games, Activities, and Recipes

David C. King

WILEY

John Wiley & Sons, Inc.

New York • Chichester • Weinheim • Brisbane • Singapore • Toronto

FAIRVIEW BRANCH
SANTA MONICA PUBLIC LIBRARY

This text is printed on acid-free paper.

Copyright © 1997 by Roundtable Press, Inc. and David C. King
Published by John Wiley & Sons, Inc.

A Roundtable Press Book
Directors: Marsha Melnick and Susan E. Meyer
Design concept: Barbara Hall
Design: Michaelis/Carpelis Design Assoc., Inc.

Illustrations © 1997 by Bobbie Moore

The photographs on pages 1, 56, 62, and 90 are courtesy of the New York Public Library Picture Collection.

The photograph on page 22 is courtesy of the Kansas Collection, University of Kansas Libraries.

All rights reserved. Published simultaneously in Canada.

Reproduction or translation of any part of this work beyond that permitted by Section 107 or 108 of the 1976 United States Copyright Act without the permission of the copyright owner is unlawful. Requests for permission or further information should be addressed to the Permissions Department, John Wiley & Sons, Inc.

Library of Congress Cataloging-in-Publication Data
King, David C.
    Pioneer days : discover the past with fun
  projects, games, activities, and recipes / David C. King :
  illustrations by Bobbie Moore.
                    p. cm. — (American kids in history ™ series)
    Includes index.
    ISBN 0-471-16169-1 (acid-free paper)
    1. Frontier and pioneer life—West (U.S.)—Study and teaching-
  -Activity programs. 2. Pioneer children—West (U.S.)—Study and
  teaching—Activity programs. 3. West (U.S.)—Social life and
  customs—Study and teaching—Activity programs. I. Moore, Bobbie,
  ill. II. Title. III. Series
  F596.K558   1997

  978í.02—dc21   96-37495

Printed in the United States of America
10 9 8 7 6 5 4 3 2 1

I would like to dedicate this book to my wife Sharon
for sharing the adventure and fun of exploring
our nation's history.

ACKNOWLEDGMENTS

Special thanks to the many people who made this book possible,
including: Kara N. Raezer, Joanne Palmer, and the editorial staff of the
Professional and Trade Division, John Wiley & Sons, Inc.; Susan E. Meyer and the
staff of Roundtable Press, Inc.; Marianne Palladino and Irene Carpelis of
Michaelis/Carpelis Design; Sharon Flitterman-King and Diane Ritch for craft expertise;
Rona Tuccillo for picture research; Steven Tiger, librarian, and the students of
the Roe-Jan Elementary School, Hillsdale, New York; and, for research
assistance, the staff members of the Great Barrington Public Library,
the Atheneum (Pittsfield, Massachusetts), Old Sturbridge Village, and
the Farmers Museum, Cooperstown, New York.

CONTENTS

INTRODUCTION 1

   MOVING WEST 1

   THE BUTLER FAMILY 2

   THE PROJECTS AND ACTIVITIES 3

CHAPTER ONE: SPRING 5

   MAKING THE CABIN A HOME 6

      Spongeware Clay Pot 7

      Air-Dried Flowers 8

   SPRINGTIME MEALS 12

      Hasty Pudding 13

      Johnnycakes 14

   FRONTIER KNOW-HOW 16

      Finding Direction 17

      Cricket Thermometer 19

      Knot This Way 20

   SAVE IT AND SEW IT 21

      Patchwork Picture 22

   SIMPLE PLEASURES 26

      Jumping Jack 27

      Thaumatrope 30

CHAPTER TWO: SUMMER 31

   SUMMER COOLERS 32

      Hay-Time Switchel 33

      Old-Time Lemonade 34

Strawberry Shrub 35
Homemade Soda Pop 36
FRIENDLY NEIGHBORS 38
African Trade Beads 39
Woven Mat 41
FAIR FUN 44
The Game of Marbles 45
LEARNING FROM THE NATIVE AMERICANS 48
Hopi Kachina Doll 49
Apache Scroll 51
Navajo Sandpainting 54

CHAPTER THREE: AUTUMN 57
AUTUMN DELIGHTS 58
Apple Butter 59
Spoon Bread 61
Roasted Pumpkin Seeds 63
HARVEST DECORATIONS 65
Cornhusk Doll 66
Halloween Ghosts 69
TREASURES FROM THE SOUTHWEST 71
Tortillas 71
TIME FOR TOYS 73
The Magic Wallet 74
Wood Choppers 76
Canada Goose Whirligig 78

CHAPTER FOUR: WINTER 81

   HOLIDAY PREPARATIONS 82

      Pinecone Angel 83

      Salt Dough Ornaments 84

      Ojo de Dios 87

   HOLIDAY GIFTS 89

      Silhouette Portrait 90

      Picture Frame 92

      Seminole Patchwork 93

      Leaf-Print Wrapping Paper 96

   EVENING FUN 98

      Tangram 99

      Folk Art Checkerboard and Game 101

      Beanbag Target Game 103

GLOSSARY 107

BIBLIOGRAPHY 115

INDEX 117

INTRODUCTION

Moving West

During the 1800s, American pioneers moved farther and farther west, exploring the land and expanding the U.S. frontier. They cleared the forests, plowed and planted fields for crops, and built log cabins.

Pioneer families faced a hard life. They were in constant danger of floods or droughts, fires, storms, and accidents or disease. They worked with hand tools and cooked over open fires in stone fireplaces. There were no machines to make work easier or faster. A trip to a general store in town to buy the few items they could not make was a special treat.

Some pioneers found that frontier life was too hard or too lonely, and they headed back to the more settled life of the East. But most stayed on. Slowly, they replaced their crude log cabins with comfortable houses and turned rough sheds into sturdy barns. Trading posts grew into towns, with stores, churches, and a school.

For kids, life on the frontier was a combination of hard work and adventure. Boys and girls learned from their parents the skills they needed. In pioneer times men and women often did different types of work. Boys aged ten and older worked in the fields with their fathers and hunted or fished to add to the

family's food supply. Girls helped their mothers make and mend clothing, cook and bake, and preserve foods for the winter months. Kids also learned to read and write at home, as one-room schools were rare at first on the frontier.

Pioneer life was not all hard work. The frontier itself was a whole new world to explore. Pioneer kids met other kids from all parts of the East or from other countries. They found time for swimming, picnics, social gatherings with neighbors, and for playing with toys and games they had made themselves.

The Butler Family

The Butlers are not a real family, but their story shows what life was like for pioneer families. This book follows the Butlers through the year 1843.

In 1840, the Butlers and their children, Samuel and Elizabeth, called Liz, sold their farm in central New York State and headed west. A three-month journey carried them into land that would one day be the northeastern part of the state of Kansas, near the Missouri border. They bought land for their new homestead on the banks of a stream called Cotters Creek, about fifteen miles from a trading settlement on the Santa Fe Trail called Council Grove.

For the family's first winter at Cotters Creek, Lucas Butler built a rough lean-to made of boards supported at one end by poles. He also cleared land for the first crops and started building a log cabin. With help from young Sam and some neighbors, the family was able to move into the cabin late in 1842. Amanda Butler shared her husband's belief that the family could build a better future on the frontier. She was delighted with the beautiful wooded land around Cotters Creek.

Twelve-year-old Samuel Butler was excited about living on the edge of an untamed wilderness. Sam helped his father in the farm fields and had a daily round of chores. He raked ashes from the fireplace, carried water from the well, and milked the cows twice a day from spring to autumn.

Nine-year-old Liz Butler had not been happy about leaving New York and all her friends. And she had hated the first shivering winter in the lean-to. But everything changed when they moved into the cabin and she helped her mother decorate their new home. She also was learning how to cook and bake, how to make butter and cheese, and how to sew cotton cloth into new clothing. Her everyday chores were to wash dishes; gather eggs; feed the chickens, geese, and pigs; and weed the kitchen garden.

The Projects and Activities

In this book you'll follow Liz and Sam through the year 1843, and do many of the things that pioneer kids did. Like them, you'll make things by hand, like a painted clay pot and a cornhusk doll. You'll also make your own toys and games and try pioneer recipes.

As you do these projects, activities, and recipes, the past will come alive. And you'll discover what it was like to be an American kid in pioneer times.

CHAPTER ONE

SPRING

PROJECTS

SPONGEWARE
CLAY POT

AIR-DRIED FLOWERS

HASTY PUDDING

JOHNNYCAKES

FINDING DIRECTION

CRICKET
THERMOMETER

KNOT THIS WAY

PATCHWORK PICTURE

JUMPING JACK

THAUMATROPE

Farming on the frontier began in the spring. As soon as the frost was out of the ground, Sam Butler helped his father hitch up the team of horses to begin plowing the fields. The Butlers' main crops were grains, especially corn and wheat. Closer to the cabin, they planted vegetables that were easy to store for the winter, like potatoes, pumpkins, and squash.

Spring was also the time when new animals were born. Liz and Sam had fun keeping track of new baby chicks, lambs, and piglets, and giving them names from the Bible. Sam and his father washed the grown sheep and sheared off the wool, which Mrs. Butler and Liz would later spin into yarn. As soon as the grass turned green, Sam milked the two cows twice a day and dairying began. From spring to autumn, Liz helped her mother preserve the milk by churning it into butter and by making cheese.

MAKING THE CABIN A HOME

By the spring of 1843, the family had been in the cabin for four months. Mrs. Butler was eager to make the raw cabin a comfortable home. She gathered brightly colored wildflowers and dried them. She arranged them in vases and jugs to decorate the cabin. She also asked the family to make the pottery they would use to store food and other items.

The most common pottery was a coarse form called earthenware. Earthenware jugs and crocks (thick pots or jars) were strong and easy to clean, so they could be used again and again. In the East, most earthenware was made by professional potters. Since there were no potters on the frontier, pioneer families like the Butlers made their own crocks and jugs.

Early in the spring, Mr. Butler found a bed of clay along the banks of Cotters Creek. It looked just right for making crocks for storing

butter and cheese. He invited Liz and Sam to use some of the clay to make smaller items for serving food at the table.

Without a special pottery oven they had to harden their earthenware more slowly over an open fire. With the pottery placed on stones around the fire, it took four days before the clay hardened into earthenware.

PROJECT SPONGEWARE CLAY POT

In this project you'll be using self-hardening clay, which is available at most discount department stores, as well as craft and hobby shops. The same stores will have fast-drying acrylic paints for decorating your pots.

You'll use a technique from the 1800s called sponge painting to decorate your pot. The finished spongeware pot makes an attractive container for the dried flowers you'll make in the next project.

MATERIALS

several sheets of newspaper
ruler
waxed paper
masking tape
1 to 2 pounds of self-hardening clay
old table knife
craft stick or tongue depressor
medium paintbrush (about ½ inch)
acrylic or poster paints: white, and your choice of a
   second, darker color
small dish
small piece of sponge

1. Spread newspaper over your work area. Place a 2-foot length of waxed paper on top of the newspaper and hold it in place with masking tape.

2. Read the directions on the container of clay. Work the clay with your hands to make it softer and easy to shape.

3. Use the table knife to cut off enough clay to make a base for your pot. Shape the base to be a circle about 4½ inches in diameter (the length of a line drawn through the center of the circle) and about ⅜ inch thick. Flatten it with the heel of your hand. Use the craft stick to make the top as smooth and flat as possible.

4. Roll out a piece of clay into a rope ¼ to ½ inch thick and long enough to fit completely around the top of the base. (You may find it easier to make two shorter ropes and join them by pinching the ends.) Shape the rope into a loop and pinch the ends, then wrap the loop around the top of the base.

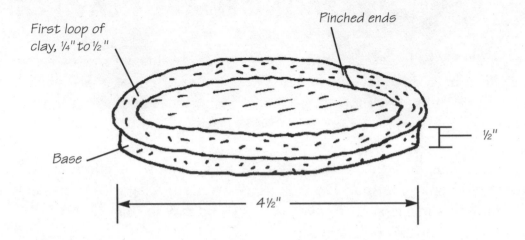

First loop of
clay, ¼" to ½"

Pinched ends

Base

½"

4½"

5. Make more loops and add them to build up the sides to a height of 4 inches or more. Stop adding loops when you like the way your pot looks. As you build the sides, use your fingers and the craft stick to smooth both the inside and the outside of the pot and make the seams invisible.

6. Add handles by making two smaller ropes, about 1¹¹⁄₂₂ inches long. Bend the ropes into a slight curve and pinch the ends to lie flat against the sides of the pot. Use scraps of clay to hold the handles in place. The handles will be stronger if they are flat against the sides.

7. Allow the clay to dry completely according to the directions on the package.

8. When the clay is dry, use the brush to paint the entire pot, inside and out, with a base coat of white paint. Allow the paint to dry.

9. Pour a little of the second paint color into the dish. Dip the piece of sponge into the paint and squeeze out the excess paint.

10. Gently dab the sponge on the pot. Continue around the outside of the pot. Redip the sponge now and then, but always squeeze out the extra paint. You will quickly see that you don't need much paint. Cover the entire outside of the pot with the spongeware pattern. Some of the base color will show through and around the sponged-on color; this creates the spongeware pattern.

11. Allow the paint to dry, and your spongeware pot is ready to use.

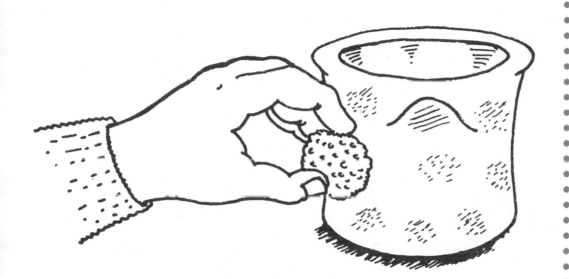

Some of the simplest and most durable American pottery was called stoneware, or salt glaze. This strong, heavy pottery was popular from the late 1700s to the late 1800s. The potter painted a cobalt blue design on the pot, then fired it in a special pottery oven called a kiln. When the fire was at its hottest, the potter threw in handfuls of salt. This salt glaze technique created a beautiful tan or light gray finish. Crocks and jugs made by this method in the 1800s are now collectors' items and can be seen in museums throughout the country.

PROJECT AIR-DRIED FLOWERS

Air-drying flowers by hanging them in bunches is the easiest way to preserve them. They'll keep their shape and much of their color for a year or more. Pick blossoms just before they reach full bloom. The best time for picking is mid- to late morning, after the dew has dried.

You can pick wildflowers and garden flowers from spring to autumn. If you pick from someone's garden, or you want wildflowers that are on private property, *always* ask permission, and take only as much as you need. You can often find wildflowers along the roadside, but keep in mind that it is against the law to pick wildflowers in parks. Work with a partner to share the fun of collecting, preserving, and arranging your flowers.

MATERIALS

4 different kinds of flowers, each with 6 to 8
   blossoms, stems, and leaves
scissors with rounded or blunt tips
basket or large grocery bag
several sheets of newspaper
ruler
string
closet clothes rod or laundry drying rack
two 8-inch-long pieces of ½-inch-wide satin ribbon
2 small vases

1. Look for four plants with clusters of tiny blossoms, such as baby's breath, lavender, heather, and goldenrod. Use the scissors to cut straight across the stem, far enough down so that you have some leaves as well as blossoms. Place the flowers carefully in the basket, blossom side down.

2. Back indoors, spread newspaper over your work area. Empty your basket of flowers. Sort the plants into the four kinds you have chosen.

3. Cut a piece of string about 8 inches long for each of the four bunches. Tie a string around the stems of each bunch so that the string is tight enough to hold the bunch together, but not so tight that it cuts into the stems.

4. Use the ends of the string to hang the bunches, blossom side down, in a warm, dry place. The clothes rod in a closet works perfectly. Give the bunches enough space so they are not touching each other. Allow 4 weeks to dry.

5. After the blossoms have dried, untie the bunches and spread them on more sheets of

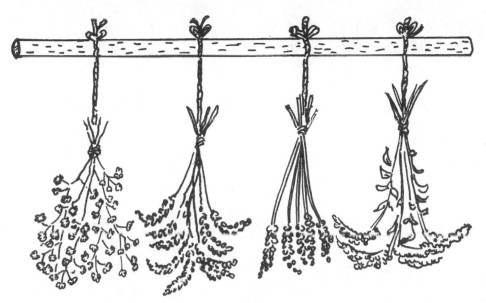

Pioneer families collected wild herbs and also grew their own in small kitchen gardens. They air-dried bunches of herbs, like dill, rosemary, basil, and peppermint, by hanging them from the beams of the cooking area or kitchen. The dried herbs were handy for cooking and filled the home with a mixture of pleasant scents.

newspaper. Handling the flowers gently and as little as possible, arrange them in two bouquets. For each bouquet, choose colors and shapes that look attractive to you. The two bouquets can be the same or very different from each other.

6. Tie each bouquet with a piece of string. Cut off the dangling ends of string. Wrap a piece of ribbon around each bouquet to cover the string, and tie the ribbon in a bow.

7. Place the bouquets in small vases and display.

SPRINGTIME MEALS

Making pottery and preserving wildflowers were only a small part of the Butler family's busy springtime work. As soon as Sam and his father finished plowing and planting one field, they moved on to the next. They also worked on turning the old lean-to into a barn and digging a root cellar for storing vegetables and fruit for the winter.

Liz and her mother spent part of each spring day in the dairy, a shed attached to the cabin where milk was kept. They churned some of the milk into butter and made some into cheese. There was also fleece (the coat of wool sheared from sheep) to spin into yarn and clothing to be sewn or mended.

With this busy schedule, Mrs. Butler sometimes made meals that were quick and easy. There were

no frozen foods in 1843, of course, and no canned or packaged foods either. Every meal had to be made from scratch, so the pioneer versions of fast food were not very speedy.

PROJECT HASTY PUDDING

This recipe and the next one will let you taste the kind of hearty meals that pioneer kids ate. Hasty pudding can provide a stick-to-your-ribs breakfast or can be eaten at any time. Leftover hasty pudding is also good fried.

INGREDIENTS
4 cups water
1 teaspoon salt
1 cup cornmeal (white or yellow)
maple syrup

EQUIPMENT
large saucepan with lid
mixing spoon
adult helper

MAKES
4 to 6 servings

1. Put the water and salt in a saucepan.

2. Ask your adult helper to heat the water and salt to a boil in the covered saucepan.

3. When the water is boiling briskly, sprinkle in the cornmeal, a little at a time. Stir constantly as you add the cornmeal to keep lumps from forming.

4. Lower the heat, cover the saucepan, and simmer for 1 hour. Stir the mixture every few minutes so that it won't stick to the pan. The pudding is ready when it is about as thick as oatmeal.

5. Serve the pudding hot with plenty of maple syrup.

 **JOHNNYCAKES**

Johnnycakes were a favorite pioneer quick food which could be taken to the fields for the midday meal. Try making your own johnnycakes.

INGREDIENTS

1 cup cornmeal (white, if possible)
1 teaspoon salt
1 tablespoon butter
1 tablespoon sugar
1 cup water
½ cup milk
vegetable oil or shortening
maple syrup

EQUIPMENT

mixing bowl
saucepan with lid
mixing spoon
paper towel
pancake griddle or frying pan
pancake turner
adult helper

MAKES

4 servings

1. Place the cornmeal, salt, butter, and sugar in a mixing bowl.

2. Ask an adult to boil the water in a covered saucepan and pour it into the bowl.

3. Add the milk to the bowl. Mix thoroughly with a spoon to make a smooth, thick batter. (If the mixture becomes too thick, stir in a little warm water.)

4. Use the paper towel to cover the griddle and pancake turner with a light coat of oil.

5. Ask your adult helper to heat the pan. The surface is hot enough when a drop of water bounces. Reduce the heat to medium.

6. Drop the batter by spoonfuls onto the hot griddle, like you would with pancake batter. Use the pancake turner to press each spoonful flat (about ½ inch thick).

7. Cook the cakes two at a time over medium heat for about 5 minutes on each side. The cakes should be crisp and slightly brown when done. Flip them a second time, if necessary.

8. Serve the cakes hot with maple syrup.

Cornmeal

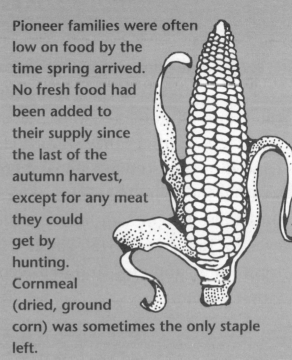

Pioneer families were often low on food by the time spring arrived. No fresh food had been added to their supply since the last of the autumn harvest, except for any meat they could get by hunting. Cornmeal (dried, ground corn) was sometimes the only staple left.

Settlers called cornmeal Indian meal because the colonists (people who settled in America before it became the United States) learned about corn from Native Americans. Native Americans were given the name Indians by the first explorers to the New World, who originally had been looking for India.

FRONTIER KNOW-HOW

When Sam and his father paused in the fields for their midday meal, Mr. Butler used the time to teach him a few things about living on the frontier. Sometimes they studied cloud patterns and wind direction so that Sam could begin to predict the weather they could expect in the next day or two. Mr. Butler also taught Sam how to build a lean-to if he ever got lost, how to find edible wild foods and fresh water, and how to find directions when traveling.

PROJECT FINDING DIRECTION

When you're trying to find compass directions, you can figure out all four directions if you can find one. For example, if you know which direction is north, you know that south is the opposite direction, west is to the left of north, and east is to the right. You can use the following frontier know-how to find direction during the day or night. Try both methods.

MATERIALS
small stick
2 small stones
watch or clock
string, about 30 inches long
compass (optional)

METHOD 1: Directions by the Sun

1. On a bright, sunny day, place the stick in the ground so that it stands straight up. Notice where the shadow falls. Place a stone at the outer tip of the shadow.

2. Wait 1 hour and place the second stone at the tip of the new shadow.

3. Stretch the string between the two stones. The string should run from east to west, with the second stone to the east. The stick should be south of the string.

4. Check your results by using the compass. Stand near the string with the compass and face the stick for your reading.

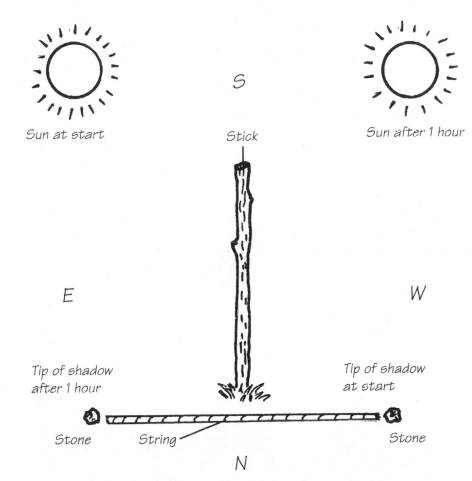

Sun at start

S

Stick

Sun after 1 hour

E

W

Tip of shadow
after 1 hour

Tip of shadow
at start

Stone

String

Stone

N

METHOD 2: Directions by the Stars

1. On a clear spring night ask an adult to help you locate the Big Dipper in the night sky.

2. Imagine a line running along the front edge of the dipper. Extend that line straight from the top of the dipper to a bright star. That star is Polaris, the North Star. Polaris is located almost directly above the North Pole of the earth, so when you face Polaris you are facing north. You can then find the other directions: east, west, and south.

3. Check to make sure you have found Polaris by looking for the Little Dipper. Polaris should be at the end of the dipper's handle.

4. Double-check your results by using the compass.

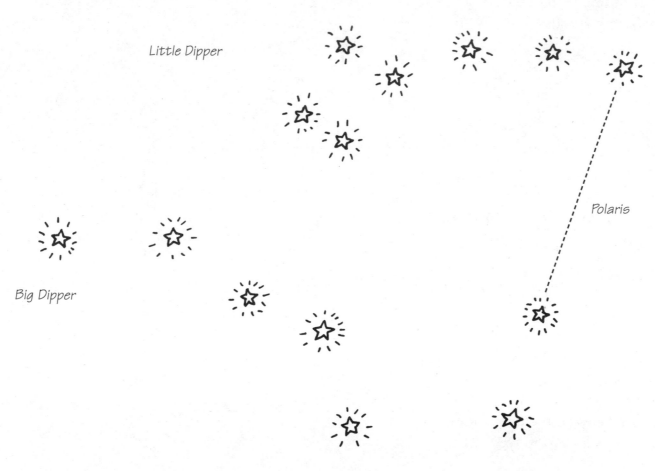

Little Dipper

Polaris

Big Dipper

PROJECT CRICKET THERMOMETER

Insects can give you some amazing clues about temperature. When the temperature drops to 48°F, for example, grasshoppers cannot fly. If the temperature drops 8° more, all insects stop chirping or buzzing.

There are several different ways to use the chirping of crickets to find out what the outdoor temperature is. Test out the two methods described here with an adult outside on a spring evening. The second method is easier, but might not be quite as accurate.

MATERIALS
watch with a second hand
pencil
scrap paper
outdoor thermometer
adult helper

METHOD 1

1. Listen carefully to the crickets' chirping until you are sure you can single out the chirps of one cricket.

2. Have your helper time you with the second hand on the watch while you count the number of chirps the cricket makes in exactly 60 seconds. Write the number on a piece of scrap paper.

3. Subtract 40 from the number of chirps. Divide the answer by 4, then add 50 to that number to determine the temperature. For example, if you count 68 chirps, subtract 40 to get 28, divide by 4 to get 7, and add 50 to get a temperature of 57°F.

4. Check your results with the outdoor thermometer.

METHOD 2

1. Have your helper time you while you count the number of chirps in exactly 14 seconds.

2. Add 40 to the number of chirps and you have the temperature. For example, if there are 17 chirps in 14 seconds, adding 40 to 17 means a temperature of 57°F. Does method 2 work? Which method works better?

3. Check your results with the outdoor thermometer.

 **KNOT THIS WAY**

There are many different kinds of knots, and some of them have special purposes. Pioneers used a knot called a clove hitch to hold logs together, and they made a lasso (a long rope with a changeable noose used for roping cattle and horses on the frontier) with a running bowline knot. One of the easiest and most useful of all knots is the square knot. It is very strong, easy to untie, and you can learn it in a few minutes. (In fact, when you tie your shoelaces, you are tying half of a square knot.)

Practice the square knot a few times, and before long you won't even have to think about how to do it. You'll be surprised at how often it comes in handy, not just for projects, but for everyday things like tying packages.

MATERIALS

heavy string, twine, or yarn (about 10 inches long)

1. Tie a knot the way you do when tying your shoes, by looping one end of the string under the other.

2. Tie a second knot, going the other way as shown in the picture. When you see the figure eight form, you know you have it.

3. Pull the ends tight. Try tugging on the ends and you will see that the knot will not loosen. And yet, you can untie it in a second.

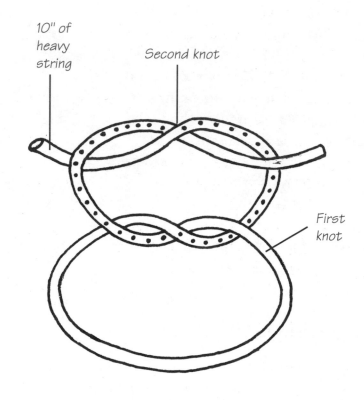

10" of heavy string

Second knot

First knot

Square Knot

Dotted line shows the figure eight.

SAVE IT AND SEW IT

In the same way Sam learned from his father, Liz was gaining a valuable education from her mother. She learned and practiced every detail of making cloth and turning it into clothing. Mrs. Butler also taught her how to make cheese, and how to know which herbs to use as medicine, and how to prepare a meal in iron kettles over an open fire.

For Liz, almost every day's work included practice in sewing, learning a new stitch, or figuring out a design. She not only helped make the family's clothing, but she and her mother also made quilts, pillows, towels, and more.

In the spring of 1843, Liz and her mother began working on a quilt. Because cotton cloth was expensive, they had been saving every scrap from worn-out clothing and bedding. They planned to make the quilt by cutting some of the scraps into squares, rectangles, and triangles, then sewing them together in a colorful pattern. Using scraps in this way is called patchwork. A number of patches sewn together into a square design is called a block. Their finished patchwork quilt

would be made up of about forty blocks sewn to a plain backing and stuffed with goose feathers and down.

Fitting different-colored patches into a design sometimes made Liz feel a little dizzy. But late in the afternoon, as supper simmered over the fire, sewing the patches was relaxing, pleasant work.

Bees

Since colonial times, American women often sewed their quilts at quilting bees. A number of women would gather together to work, exchange news, and gossip. Sometimes the entire family joined in these social occasions.

People also worked together in bees to do such tasks as peeling apples, husking corn, or raising barns. Pioneers carried these practices westward, and the gatherings became an important time for meeting neighbors, sharing news, and turning work into fun. The bee always included a huge feast, followed by singing and dancing.

PROJECT PATCHWORK PICTURE

In this project, you'll copy a popular pioneer quilt pattern called Memory Wreath. It was also known as Crown of Thorns and Georgetown Circle. Instead of sewing patches together to make a block, you'll be working with construction paper. You can hang the colorful finished pattern on the wall of your room.

MATERIALS

ruler
pencil
sheet of red construction paper
scissors
2 sheets of blue construction paper
12-inch square of white poster board or cardboard
white glue

1. Use the ruler and pencil to mark off four 2-inch squares on the red construction paper. Cut out the 4 squares.

2. Use the ruler and pencil to draw a line from one corner to the opposite corner on one of the squares to create 2 triangles. Cut out the triangles. Repeat this with the other 3 squares to make a total of 8 red triangles. Set these aside.

3. Repeat steps 1 and 2 with a sheet of blue construction paper, but this time make six 2-inch squares and cut them into 12 triangles. Make a separate pile of these.

4. With pencil and ruler, mark six 3-inch squares on a second sheet of blue construction paper. Cut out the 6 squares. Set 4 of the squares aside. (These will form the four corners of your pattern.)

5. Cut the 2 remaining large blue squares into triangles. This will give you 4 large blue triangles.

6. On the 12-inch square of white poster board, use the ruler and pencil to mark a dot on all four sides exactly 3 inches from each corner. Connect the dots with a pencil line as shown. This gives you a grid for fitting all the triangles and squares in place.

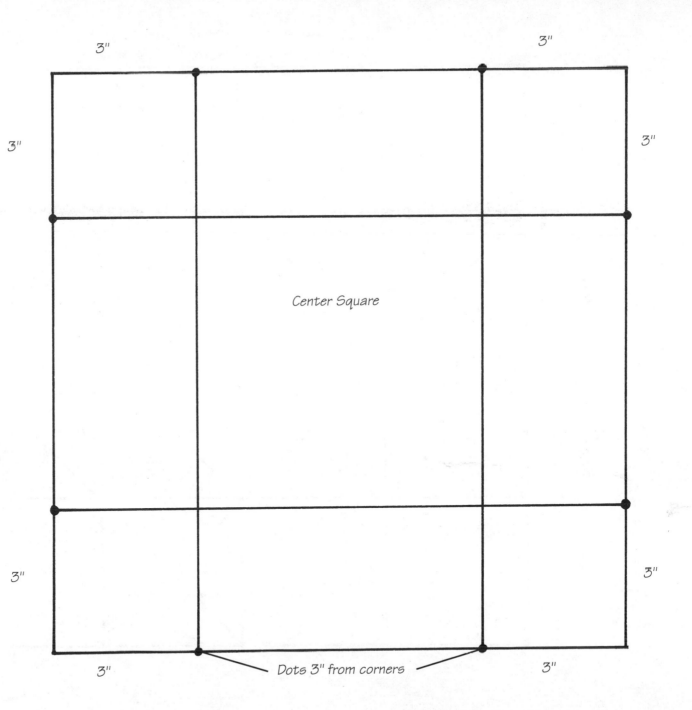

3" 3"

3" 3"

Center Square

3" 3"

3" 3"

Dots 3" from corners

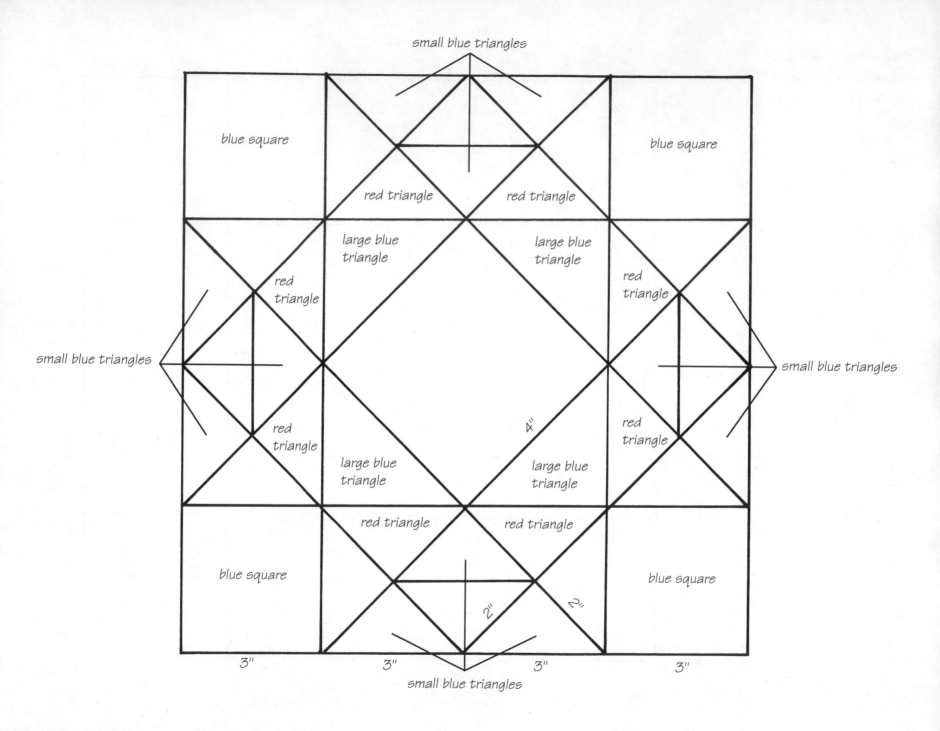

small blue triangles

blue square

blue square

red triangle

red triangle

large blue
triangle

large blue
triangle

red
triangle

red
triangle

small blue triangles

small blue triangles

red
triangle

red
triangle

4"

large blue
triangle

large blue
triangle

red triangle

red triangle

blue square

blue square

2"

2"

3"

3"

3"

3"

small blue triangles

7. Put each of the 4 large blue squares in place at each corner. Put a bead (line) of glue around the edges of each square and a dot of glue in the middle, and glue the squares to the poster board.

8. Fit each of the 4 large blue triangles inside the square in the center of the poster board so that their short ends align with the sides of the square. When the triangles are in the right position, glue them in place.

9. Position the 8 red triangles so that the base (long edge) of each is against the side of a large blue triangle. Glue the red triangles to the poster board.

10. Position 4 of the small blue triangles in between the red ones. Glue them in place.

11. Fit the remaining 8 blue triangles against the sides of the poster board. Glue these remaining pieces in place, and your patchwork pattern is ready to display.

Changing Technology

In the mid-1840s, a New England inventor named Elias Howe was struggling to create a machine that would sew. Howe's sewing machine, greatly improved by Isaac M. Singer in the 1850s, produced a revolution in the textile industry. Machines could produce clothing more quickly and cheaply than people sewing by hand. By the 1880s, sewing machines were inexpensive enough for most households to own one.

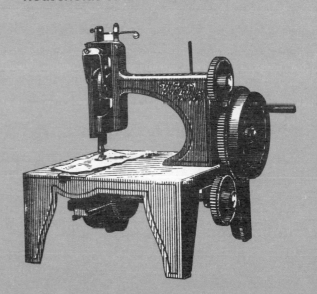

SIMPLE PLEASURES

Liz spent her days sewing, mending, spinning, weaving, cooking, baking, and cleaning. Sam's spring days were just as busy. He plowed, hoed, and weeded the fields, cleaned the stalls, worked on the half-finished barn, chopped wood for the fireplace, and carried water. Even with all that work, there was still time for fun. By late spring, the children could hunt for wild berries, mushrooms, honeybee hives, and other wild foods. On Sunday afternoons, they played with Sunday toys or games that would not disturb the quiet of the Sabbath, the day of rest.

Like other pioneer children, Liz and Sam made most of their own toys, often with some help from a parent. They were fascinated by any toy that moved. They made a spinning toy with the fancy name of "thaumatrope," and they made jumping jacks and put on their own puppet shows.

PROJECT JUMPING JACK

Jumping jacks are simple hand puppets that can be made to jump or dance when you pull on a central string. While pioneer kids made theirs from any scraps of wood they could find, you'll make yours out of poster board. The toy is easy to make, and part of the fun is deciding how to decorate it. Jumping jacks can be made to look like soldiers, dancers, acrobats, clowns, pirates, or famous people. Work with a friend to make different kinds.

MATERIALS
pencil
white poster board
ruler
scissors
paper hole punch
awl or compass point (to be used by adult only)
crayons or markers
scraps of fabric or lace, buttons, beads, etc.
white glue
string or heavy thread
four ½-inch brass paper fasteners
adult helper

1. Look at the model on page 28, and draw the body, leg, and arm on the white poster board. Use a ruler to make the pieces in the lengths shown. Cut out the 3 pieces.

A Jumping Jack Craze

Jumping jacks, called *pantins* in French, were invented in France about 1740. A pantin fad swept across France. The city of Paris even tried, without success, to pass a law banning the toy because some people made comical pantins of the king and his court. The fad of making pantins spread to the United States, where the figures were called jumping jacks, and they became one of the most popular toys of the 1800s.

2. Make a second arm and leg by tracing around your cutout pieces on the remaining poster board. Cut out the second arm and leg.

3. With the pencil, mark five dots for making small holes as shown in the drawing. Then mark eight dots for making larger holes.

4. Use the paper punch to make the eight large holes. Ask an adult helper to make the five small holes with the awl or the compass point.

5. Decide what kind of figure you want to make—clown, ballerina, king or queen, or anything else. Decorate the pieces of your jumping jack with crayons or markers. Use scraps of fabric to make a turban, crown, or hat, and to make a skirt or pants and a top. Attach these pieces to the jumping jack with the white glue. Add other bits of decoration, such as beads, lace, or glitter. If you covered up any holes, re-punch them.

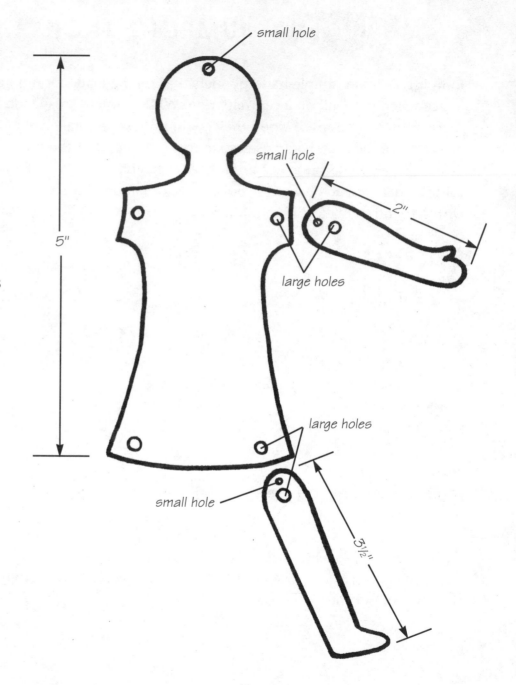

small hole

small hole

2"

large holes

large holes

5"

small hole

3½"

6. Run a 6-inch piece of string or heavy thread through the hole in the top of the head. Tie the ends of the string together in a double knot. (You will use this string to hold the jumping jack.)

7. Attach the arms and legs to the body by pushing the paper fasteners through the large holes (with the prongs in the back of the

figure). Press back the prongs, but not too tightly—the arms and legs should swing freely.

8. Place the jumping jack on your worktable. Put the arms and legs in the down position. Run a piece of string through the two small holes at the shoulders. Tie each end in a firm knot. Repeat with the legs.

9. Tie a piece of string to the center of the string that connects the arms. Make a double knot or a square knot. Run the string down to the string that connects the legs and tie a knot there. Extend the string about 3 inches past the bottom of the feet. Cut the string and tie the end in a double knot.

10. Hold the string above the jumping jack's head in one hand. With the other hand, pull down on string at the bottom to make the figure jump or dance.

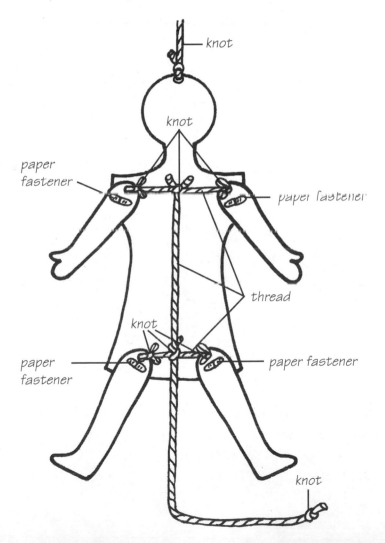

knot

paper fastener

knot

paper fastener

paper fastener

thread

knot

paper fastener

knot

fabric

lace

beads

fabric

PROJECT THAUMATROPE

The thaumatrope is a simple toy that creates optical illusions. In the days before television and radio, people used this kind of toy as part of an evening's entertainment. Some of the toys were quite complicated. They were always given scientific-sounding names, like "thaumatrope," "chromatrope," and "phenakistoscope." (*Thauma* is a Greek word meaning wonder or miracle.)

In this project, the spinning disk you make will create the illusion of a fish in a bowl. You can make your own version of the same idea: a prisoner behind bars, a sailing ship in a bottle, a bird in a cage, or any other combination.

MATERIALS

drawing compass
heavy white poster board or cardboard
scissors
awl or compass point (to be used by adult only)
pencil
crayons or magic markers
two 16-inch pieces of string
two 4-inch sticks or pieces of doweling
adult helper

1. Use the compass to outline a circle on the poster board about 3 inches in diameter. Cut out the circle.

Side 1

2. Ask an adult to use the awl or compass point to punch 2 holes on opposite ends of the circle as shown.

3. Use the pencil to draw a fish on one side of the circle. On the other side, draw a fishbowl. Draw the fishbowl so that the fish on the other side is directly in the center of the bowl and fits inside the bowl.

Side 2

4. Color the drawings with crayons or markers.

5. Run one piece of string through a pair of holes on one side of the circle. Tie the ends of the string about 2 inches apart on the stick. Tie the string tight, with a double knot or square knot. Repeat with the other string and stick.

Side 3

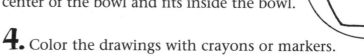

stick   stick

6. Wind the thaumatrope by twisting the sticks again and again. Then slowly pull the sticks in opposite directions. The circle will spin, creating a single picture of the fish inside the bowl.

CHAPTER TWO

SUMMER

PROJECTS

HAY-TIME SWITCHEL

OLD-TIME LEMONADE

STRAWBERRY SHRUB

HOMEMADE
SODA POP

AFRICAN TRADE
BEADS

WOVEN MAT

THE GAME OF
MARBLES

HOPI KACHINA DOLL

APACHE SCROLL

NAVAJO
SANDPAINTING

Spring slowly turned to summer on the Butler homestead. For Liz and Sam, summer was the most exciting season. In the summer the family made several trips to Council Grove to trade with settlers on wagon trains heading out the Santa Fe Trail.

The children loved the great blending of people on the town's dusty streets. They met other pioneer families, including some who had just arrived in America from Europe. They saw traders from the Mexican lands of the Southwest and small groups of Indians from several tribes who rode into town to trade.

There were also two great social gatherings that made the summer special. First came Independence Day, the nation's most popular holiday. Then, late in the summer, a fair was held in Council Grove. For Liz and Sam, both events were times to make new friends, play games, and enter contests.

SUMMER COOLERS

Before the fun of summer could begin, however, they had to complete the hot, tiring work of bringing in the hay. The Butlers joined with some of their neighbors in the task, mowing one family's hay field, then another, until all the hay was in. Fieldwork was usually done by the men, but Mrs. Butler, Liz, and all the other women pitched in. Everyone knew that they would have to have hay to feed their farm animals through the winter, so, as they said, they had to "make hay while the sun shines."

The Butlers and their neighbors began mowing hay at dawn. They moved in a line across the field, pausing only long enough for a quick, cooling drink and their midday meal. Haying was such hot, dusty work that Liz and Sam felt they could never get enough to drink. The favorite beverage for haying was a cold ginger-flavored drink called hay-time switchel. The Butlers kept their switchel cold by storing jugs of it in a shady pool in Cotters Creek.

At night, the family who owned the field being mowed that day served a hearty meal for everyone. Of course, the workers were still thirsty, so there was plenty of lemonade, another favorite drink called strawberry shrub, homemade soda pop, and, of course, hay-time switchel.

Get together with some friends and mix your own batch of switchel. For a true pioneer flavor, try drinking it cold, without ice. You'll find that it's a great thirst quencher after some hard physical activity.

INGREDIENTS

2 quarts water
1 cup sugar
½ cup molasses
⅛ cup cider vinegar
½ teaspoon ground ginger

EQUIPMENT

large saucepan with lid
wooden mixing spoon
large pitcher
adult helper

MAKES

about eight 8-ounce glassfuls

1. Ask an adult to heat 1 quart of water in a covered saucepan. When the water is hot, but not boiling, little bubbles will form on the side of the saucepan.

2. Stir in the sugar, molasses, vinegar, and ginger.

Continue stirring and heating, but don't let the mixture boil. When all the ingredients have dissolved, turn off the heat.

3. Have the adult help you remove the mixture from the stove, and let it cool until it reaches room temperature.

4. When it is cool, add the rest of the water.

5. Pour the switchel into a pitcher and chill it in a refrigerator. Serve cold.

OLD-TIME LEMONADE

If Americans had a national drink in 1843 for all the seasons, it would have been apple cider. But, during the hot summer months, lemonade was the most popular drink. Like all pioneer foods and beverages, lemonade was made from scratch. And it was made with great care to get all the flavor from the lemons and even the lemon oil in the rinds. Follow the directions, and you'll find the results are worth the work.

INGREDIENTS

4 lemons
1 cup sugar
1 quart water

EQUIPMENT

paring knife (to be used only by an adult)
cutting board
mixing bowl
saucepan with lid
mixing spoon
citrus juicer
medium bowl
strainer or cheesecloth
pitcher
adult helper

MAKES

about four 8-ounce glassfuls

1. Ask your adult helper to use a paring knife and cutting board to peel the rinds from the lemons and cut the rinds into ½-inch slices. Set the lemons aside.

2. Place the rinds in the mixing bowl and sprinkle the sugar over them. Let stand for 1 hour, so that the sugar begins to soak up the lemon oil.

3. Have the adult bring the water to a rapid boil in a covered saucepan and carefully pour the hot water over the sugared rinds.

4. Allow the mixture to cool for about 20 minutes, then remove the rinds with a mixing spoon.

5. Squeeze the lemons into the medium bowl, then pour the juice through a strainer into the sugar mixture.

6. Stir the mixture well, pour it into a pitcher, and refrigerate.

7. Serve ice cold or over ice. Add a slice of lemon for color, if you wish.

PROJECT: STRAWBERRY SHRUB

Fruit shrubs, made of fruit juice and sugar, were another favorite drink of early summer, when the first strawberries and other berries were ready to pick. You can make other kinds of tasty coolers by substituting red or black raspberries, currants, or cranberries for the strawberries.

INGREDIENTS
1 pint strawberries (fresh or frozen)
1 pint water
½ cup sugar
¼ cup lemon juice

EQUIPMENT
mixing bowl
potato masher (if available)
wooden mixing spoon
saucepan with lid
colander or cheesecloth
pitcher
adult helper

MAKES
about four 8-ounce glassfuls

1. Clean the strawberries and place them in a mixing bowl. Mash them thoroughly, using a potato masher or wooden spoon.

2. Have an adult bring the water to a boil in a covered saucepan.

3. Add the sugar and lemon juice to the boiling water and stir. Continue boiling and stirring until all the sugar has dissolved.

Ice for Drinks and Food Storage

Ice for drinks or preserving foods was a luxury until about 1830. While some Southern plantation owners and a few wealthy Northerners had icehouses, most people went without ice during the summer months.

Then, over a period of about twenty years in the early 1800s, two New Englanders, Nathaniel Wyeth and Frederic Tudor, perfected methods for cutting and storing large cakes of ice. By the early 1840s, the port of Boston was shipping 65,000 tons of ice to cities throughout the nation and the world. In Eastern cities, the icebox was becoming a standard feature in people's homes.

Pioneers could not buy ice, but they knew the methods invented by Wyeth and Tudor. They cut winter ice in large blocks, packed the blocks in sawdust, and stored them in limestone caves. The ice remained usable throughout the summer. Frontier families had not yet learned to use ice to preserve food, but some communities used their ice caves for special treats like ice cream and iced drinks.

4. Ask the adult to pour the hot sugar-and-lemon mixture over the berries. Stir the mixture well.

5. Allow the shrub to cool in the mixing bowl.

6. Place a colander over the pitcher and pour the shrub into it. Press the mixing spoon against the colander to push through as much of the mashed berries as possible.

7. Chill the shrub for 1 hour, then serve over ice in tall glasses.

 **HOMEMADE SODA POP**

Bottled soft drinks were not invented until the 1880s, but pioneers made homemade soda pop, following recipes like this one. They first made a thick syrup, then added a few ingredients to make the fizz that gave the drink a special zest. Try this recipe and see what you think of soda pop before Hires, Coca-Cola, and Dr Pepper came along.

MATERIALS
½ pint water
1 cup sugar
1 teaspoon cream of tartar
½ teaspoon vanilla extract
1 egg
cold tap water
fruit juice or root beer flavoring (optional)
½ teaspoon lemon juice
½ teaspoon bicarbonate of soda (baking soda)

EQUIPMENT
saucepan with lid
mixing spoon
medium mixing bowl
eggbeater
1-quart bottle with lid
adult helper

MAKES

about twelve 8-ounce glassfuls

1. Have your adult helper heat the water to boiling in a covered saucepan.

2. Reduce the heat to medium, and stir in the sugar and cream of tartar. Keep stirring and heating until the sugar has dissolved completely.

3. Have the adult remove the saucepan from the heat. Stir in the vanilla, then allow the mixture to cool.

4. Have the adult help you separate the egg white from the yolk. Discard the yolk and put the egg white in a medium bowl.

5. Beat the egg white with an eggbeater until the white is quite stiff. Add the egg white to the mixture in the saucepan. Stir well to blend all the ingredients.

6. Pour the mixture into the bottle. Put the lid on the bottle, and place in the refrigerator. (Don't drink this. It is your soda syrup, similar to the syrup still used in some soda fountains.)

7. To make soda pop, fill an 8-ounce glass with cold water. Stir in 2 tablespoons of syrup. For varied flavors, you can add fruit juice or root beer flavoring.

8. Add the lemon juice and bicarbonate of soda, and stir well. Serve over ice.

The Search for Fizz Drinks

People in Europe and a few places in America had long enjoyed the fizzy carbonated water that came from underground mineral springs. In the early 1800s, several different European and American inventors found ways to create artificially carbonated water. This new sparkling water was called imitation mineral water, but later became known simply as soda water. By the 1830s, soda water was becoming a favorite beverage at the popular new establishments called ice-cream parlors.

On the frontier, however, and in most rural areas, homemade soda pop was the closest people could come to carbonated beverages. Then, in 1886, a pharmacist named Hires began to bottle and sell his famous Philadelphia root beer. Within a year, two rival companies entered the business: Coca-Cola and Dr Pepper. It was not long before homemade soda pop faded into history.

FRIENDLY NEIGHBORS

Ezra and Harriet Taylor were neighbors of the Butlers. The Taylors had escaped from slavery on a Mississippi plantation and made their way to the frontier, beyond the reach of the slave laws.

The Taylors kept alive many of the crafts and traditions of their ancestors from West African kingdoms. Liz and Sam were fascinated by the handcrafted objects in the Taylors' cabin. There were delicate baskets made of grass and willow, carved wooden figures and walking sticks, a banjo, and a colorful quilt that combined African and American designs.

Harriet Taylor showed the children her collection of beads. In Africa, beads like these were used in trade or as a sign of wealth. Mrs. Taylor taught Liz and Sam how to make baskets by weaving reeds that grew in the marshes near Cotters Creek. The children thought that the baskets were beautiful.

PROJECT AFRICAN TRADE BEADS

For this project you can work with a partner to make necklaces or bracelets from the African trade beads. The beads can also be used for holiday decorations for Christmas or Kwanzaa, by forming them into small circles or longer chains for tree decorations.

MATERIALS

several sheets of newspaper
masking tape
waxed paper
1-pound package of self-hardening clay
compass point, meat skewer, or knitting needle (to be used only by an adult)
several small paintbrushes
acrylic paints or poster paints in your choice of colors
large sewing needle or rug needle
paper towel
strong string or dental floss (26 inches for a necklace, 6 to 7 inches for a bracelet)
scissors
adult helper

1. Cover your work area with newspaper. Tape a large piece of waxed paper on top to give you a smooth work surface.

2. Work the clay with your hands until it's soft and easy to mold.

3. Shape the clay into beads. Traditional African trade beads were usually an oval shape, but you can vary this by making round, square, and rectangular shapes. For a necklace, you will need 30 to 40 beads; you'll need 12 to 15 beads for a bracelet.

4. Have an adult use the compass point to make a hole through each bead for stringing. (Both the bead and the hole will shrink a little as the clay hardens.)

5. Allow 24 hours for the clay to harden (or follow the manufacturer's instructions on the package).

6. When the beads have hardened, apply a base coat of paint to each bead. The base coat can be white or any other color you choose. Allow the paint to dry.

7. To make it easier to paint designs on each bead, make a painting stand. Shape a lemon-size ball of leftover clay into a small pyramid shape.

8. Use different colors and designs to decorate each bead—straight lines, zigzags, dots, tiny triangles, or whatever else you think of. Some beads can be solid colors. Allow the paint to dry.

9. Remove the needle from the clay pyramid and wipe it clean with the paper towel. Thread the string like sewing thread through the eye of the needle.

10. String the beads by threading the needle through the hole in each bead.

11. Cut the string and tie the ends together in a double knot or square knot. Your African trade beads are ready to wear.

Stick the sharp end of the needle vertically into the clay, so that the blunt end of the needle is up. Slip a bead onto the needle and press the bead down a little so the clay pyramid holds the bead steady while you paint. You can turn the whole pyramid to paint all the way around the bead.

PROJECT WOVEN MAT

Instead of using marsh reeds for weaving like Mrs. Taylor, you can use construction paper. There are many different weaving patterns, and some of them can be very complicated. For your weaving project, you'll make a checkerboard pattern called plain weave using brown and yellow paper. Make a second mat using two other colors. Use the finished mats underneath a planter, a vase, or a cold beverage.

MATERIALS

2 sheets of construction paper: 1 yellow and 1 brown
pencil
ruler
scissors
8-by-9-inch poster board, in gray, tan, or another
    neutral color
white glue

1. Place the yellow sheet of construction paper on your work area. With pencil and ruler, draw a line across the top of the sheet 1 inch down from the top edge. This 1-inch space will be your margin.

2. Draw 11 parallel lines down the sheet from the margin to the bottom edge perpendicular to the margin. To do this, use the ruler and pencil to

mark a dot every ³/₄ inch along the margin. You should have 11 dots. Make another row of 11 dots along the bottom edge of the sheet, starting from the same side as you did for the margin dots. Then connect the dots to create 11 parallel lines running the length of the sheet.

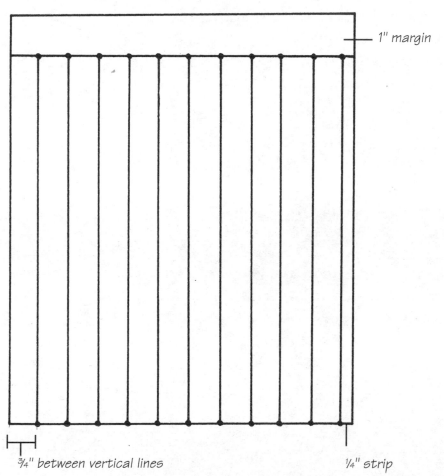

1" margin

³/₄" between vertical lines   ¹/₄" strip

Nature's Weaving Supplies

Like the early colonists, the pioneers learned to weave baskets from both Africans and Native Americans. They learned to use an amazing variety of natural materials for baskets that had different uses. Small, tightly woven baskets were made from grasses, straw, cornhusks, and even pine needles. Larger, heavier baskets were woven from different kinds of vines, willow branches, and splints cut from ash, poplar, or maple trees.

In the area of Charleston, South Carolina, Africans and their descendants made baskets from a special sweet grass. The men cut the tall sweet grass in marshes, and the women wove it into baskets of many shapes and sizes. The sweet-smelling baskets are still made in Charleston, following the traditional method. These baskets are considered to be among the finest examples of American basket weaving.

3. With the scissors, carefully cut along each of the 11 lines from the bottom of the sheet exactly to the margin. Do not cut into the margin. (You will have one very narrow, ¼-inch strip on the end. Cut this off.)

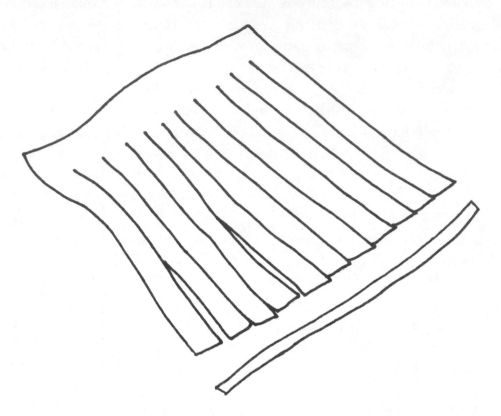

4. Use the pencil and ruler to divide the brown sheet of construction paper into 11 strips, as you did in step 2, but this time with no margin. Cut these strips all the way through, so that you have 11 separate pieces.

5. Place your sheet of yellow strips on the poster board. Center the sheet so that the edges line up with the edges of the poster board.

6. Spread glue on the back of the 1-inch margin and glue it to the poster board. (Don't glue the strips!) Gluing the margin keeps the yellow strips in place as you weave.

7. To weave, take one of the brown strips and place it under the first yellow strip, close to the margin. Weave the brown strip over the second yellow strip, then under the third, continuing over and under all the way across. Trim off the ends of the brown strip so they are even with the edges of the yellow paper.

8. Weave a second brown strip by placing it first over the first yellow strip, then under, then over, all the way across. Trim off the ends.

9. Weave the other brown strips the same way until your square is complete. You should have a neat checkerboard, or plain weave, pattern.

10. Glue the edges of all the strips to the poster board, and your woven mat is finished.

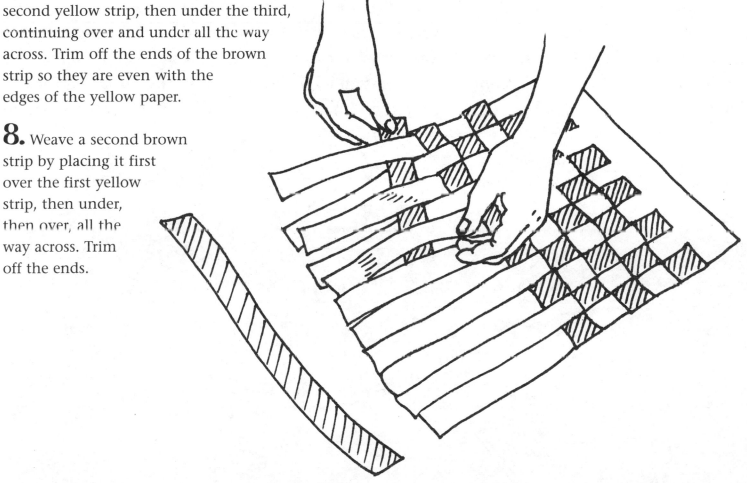

FAIR FUN

Once the haying season was over, the rest of the summer seemed almost easy to Sam and Liz. Liz continued to help her mother churn butter and make cheese in addition to her regular chores. And even though Sam complained that he spent all his time hoeing the cornfield to keep the weeds down, there were a few lazier days now. The children had time to hunt for wild berries or go for a swim in one of the deeper pools of Cotters Creek.

Best of all, they could enjoy the trips to Council Grove for July Fourth and the fair. Both Liz and Sam decided that they liked the fair best, because it lasted for three days instead of one. They also had the chance to sleep under the stars by putting their blankets on a pile of straw in the back of the wagon.

At the fair, they tried all sorts of new foods, including their first taste of buffalo meat. While they did not care much for buffalo, they did enjoy cold sherbet and soda pop. They also watched a puppet show put on by a family of traveling puppeteers, and played dozens of different games, like hopscotch and marbles.

PROJECT THE GAME OF MARBLES

There are dozens of different marble games. Here are three of the most popular from the 1800s. You'll need 2 to 4 players, a collection of marbles, and a stick or piece of chalk for drawing a line, circle, or square.

General Rules for Playing Marbles

1. Pitching or shooting the marble (also called knuckling down) is the same for all games: Place the knuckles of your index and middle fingers on the ground. Put a marble in the crook of your index finger and use your thumb to flick it across the ground by rolling it, as shown. Don't bounce it! Remember, you must keep at least one knuckle on the ground.

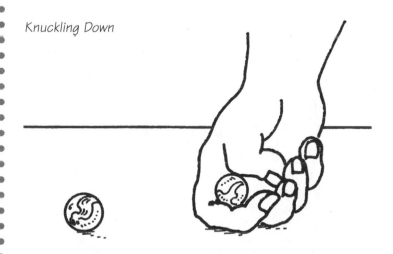

Knuckling Down

2. To decide who shoots first, draw a line about 6 feet away from the players. Each player shoots 1 marble to see who can come closest to the line without going over it. This is called lagging. The player with the best lag shoots first. If there are more than 2 players, the player who shoots the next closest to the line goes second.

Game 1: Moshie (also called Hundreds)

MATERIALS

patch of bare ground, free of grass or pebbles
yardstick
stick
marbles

1. With the heel of your shoe, dig a small round hole in the dirt, about 3 inches across and 2 inches deep. This will be called the pot.

2. Measure a distance of 6 feet from the pot and use the stick to mark a shooting line.

3. Lag to see who shoots first. The winner will be player 1.

4. Player 1 pitches a marble from behind the shooting line, trying to get it in the pot. If he

Moshie (or Hundreds)

Shooting line

Pot

misses, leave the marble where it stops until player 2 shoots. If either player puts a marble in the pot, score 10 points. But, if both players put their marbles in the pot, there is no score.

5. After the first shot, pick up any marbles and start again. Players take turns, each shooting just 1 marble. The first player to score 100 points wins the game.

Game 2: Ringer
MATERIALS
pavement
yardstick
piece of chalk
marbles

1. Draw a circle with the chalk on the pavement 8 to 10 feet in diameter.

2. Lag to see who shoots first. The winner will be player 1.

3. In the center of the circle, make an X of 13 marbles. Player 1 puts in 7 marbles. Player 2 puts in 6. Space the marbles about 2 inches apart.

Ringer

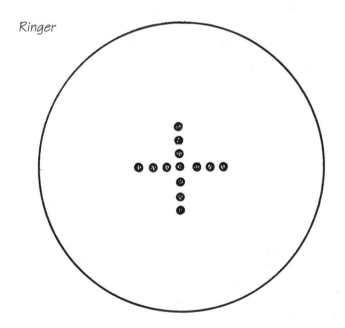

4. Player 1 shoots first, from outside the circle. The object is to knock marbles out of the circle. Player 1 keeps shooting until she fails to knock out a marble. *Note: If the shooter marble stops inside the circle, shoot it from where it stopped.*

5. Players keep taking turns until all the marbles have been knocked out of the circle. Each player keeps any marbles she knocked out.

Game 3: Bowlers
MATERIALS
pavement
yardstick
piece of chalk
marbles

1. Mark off a 2-foot square on the pavement with chalk.

2. Lag to see who shoots first. The winner will be player 1.

3. Place a marble at each corner of the square and one in the middle. Player 1 contributes 2 marbles. Player 2 puts in 3. Each marble has a number, as shown.

4. Player 1 shoots first, pitching from any corner except the corner closest to marble 1. The object

Bowlers

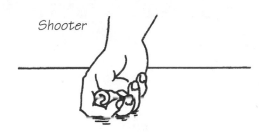
Shooter

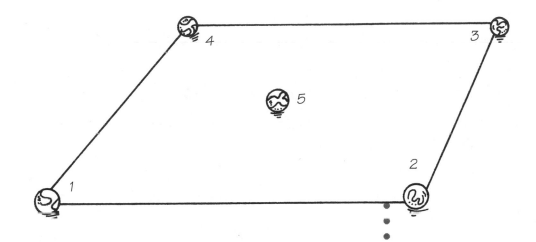

is to knock out all 5 marbles, but they must be knocked out in order, 1 through 5.

5. Player 1 pitches his second shot from wherever the shooter marble stopped. If player 1 misses, all marbles are put back in the square, and player 2 takes a turn.

6. The first player to knock out all 5 marbles without a miss is the winner.

LEARNING FROM THE NATIVE AMERICANS

Ofew days after the Butlers returned home from the fair, a trader on his way to Council Grove stopped by the cabin. He was with a wagon train on the Santa Fe Trail when a wheel came off his wagon. He had come to ask Mr. Butler to help him repair it. Mr. Butler helped fix the wheel, and then asked the trader to stay for supper and spend the night.

During supper, Liz and Sam listened spellbound to the trader's stories about the Southwest. He told them about the Hopi, Navajo, Apache, and more than twenty other tribes living in that region. As he talked, the trader unrolled a buffalo-hide scroll painted with carefully crafted pictures. He explained that the scroll described important events in Apache history. The pictures, called pictographs, were a form of writing. The paint was made from powdered plants and minerals and applied with small brushes made of twigs and animal hair.

The trader told them of another form of painting called sandpainting, which was practiced by the Navajo and Zuni. The same kind of powders were used, but

they weren't painted on. Instead, the Navajo and Zuni people carefully sprinkled the powders to make a picture used for a religious ceremony. At the end of each day, they destroyed the painting and returned the powders to nature.

As the trader prepared to leave the next morning, he gave each of the children a kachina doll from a Hopi village. He explained that the dolls were not toys. Instead, they were models of the costumed male dancers, the kachinas, who performed important religious ceremonies.

PROJECT — HOPI KACHINA DOLL

Kachina dolls are models of real kachinas, the male dancers who led important religious ceremonies in the Hopi and Zuni cultures. The ceremonies were done to bring the blessings of rain, a good corn harvest, and the general well-being of all the people. The kachinas represented the spirits of plants, birds, people, and elements of nature. Each kachina had a special name, such as wolf, eagle, owl, early morning, sun, and rattle.

For this project you'll make a slightly changed form of a kachina called Tawa, the sun. The original kachinas were carved from the root of the cottonwood tree, but yours will be made of clay. Kachina dolls usually have rather flat, or squarish, figures, so you don't have to make a completely round head and body. Kachinas also often wore a kilt, which is a kind of skirt, that extended far down the legs.

MATERIALS

several sheets of newspaper
1-pound package of self-hardening clay
craft stick or tongue depressor
drawing compass
8½-by-11-inch piece of poster board or cardboard
scissors
pencil
small piece of thick white yarn or cotton
craft glue or white glue
1 or more small paintbrushes
poster paint or acrylic paints: white, black, red, yellow, turquoise

Kachina Ceremonies

The Hopi regarded the kachinas as a link between humans and the spirits. They believed the spirits represented by the kachinas stayed in the mountains for half the year, then came to the villages during the other half. As the kachina dancers entered a village, they gave kachina dolls to the children to teach them about the symbols of their religion. Kachinas were used for curing the sick, hunting, and war (although the Hopi rarely engaged in warfare).

One group of kachinas, called the clowns, amused the villagers during religious ceremonies. If a villager had committed the sin of being a show-off, the clowns would poke fun at him. This ridicule helped support a central Hopi value: that no one should try to do better, or be more important, than other members of the community. The clowns kept people entertained during the long religious ceremonies.

1. Spread newspaper over your work surface. Work the clay with your hands to make it soft.

2. Shape a head and body wearing a kilt out of the block of clay. Use the craft stick to cut away bits of clay. Give the figure a squarish shape.

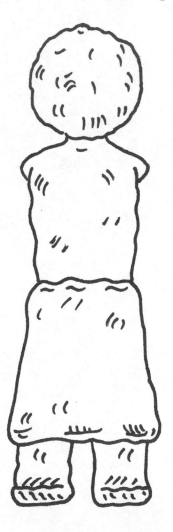

3. Cut away some clay from the base to shape the legs and feet. Make the feet thicker if your figure has trouble standing upright.

4. Shape bent arms out of the clay you have cut away. (It's not important that the arms or hands be perfectly shaped.) Use additional bits of clay to attach the arms to the body.

5. Make and attach the dancer's rattles the same way.

6. Use the compass to draw a 3-inch circle on the poster board, and cut it out. Draw the face on the circle in pencil.

7. Use the white yarn to fit around the edge of the mask. Glue it to the mask.

8. Cut 8 small triangle points from scraps of poster board and glue them to the edges of the mask as shown.

9. Decide which colors you want to use on each part of the doll. Carefully paint the mask, using the 5 colors any way that you want. Paint all of one color first, then rinse the brush and allow the paint to dry before going on to the next mask color.

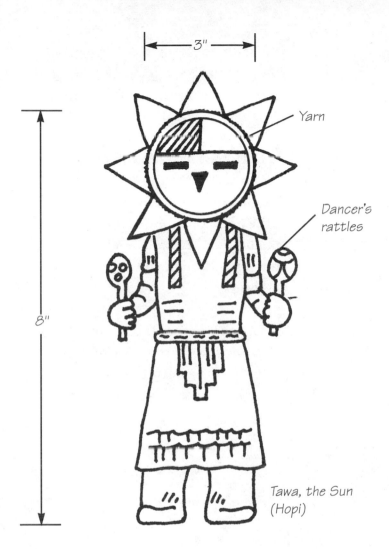

← 3" →

Yarn

Dancer's rattles

8"

Tawa, the Sun (Hopi)

10. While the paint on the mask dries, paint the body, kilt, legs, and feet of the doll in the colors chosen.

11. Glue the mask to the head, and your kachina doll is finished.

PROJECT APACHE SCROLL

Native American picture scrolls were made of deerskin or buffalo hide and tied between two poles. You'll make your scroll using brown paper and draw pictures and symbols on the scroll to tell a story. You can invent your own pictures and symbols, or copy some of the ones shown here. The story can be an event in history, happenings in your own life, or events in nature, such as the changing seasons or storms. You can even divide the story into days or months, using the sun (day:○) or moon (month:●) as symbols.

MATERIALS

scissors
ruler
heavy brown wrapping paper or a large brown grocery bag
masking tape
one-hole paper punch
pair of leather thongs (sold as shoelaces) or twine
2 straight sticks or dowels, each about 28 inches long
pencil
small paintbrush
acrylic paints or poster paints in your choice of colors
red, black, and blue felt-tip pens

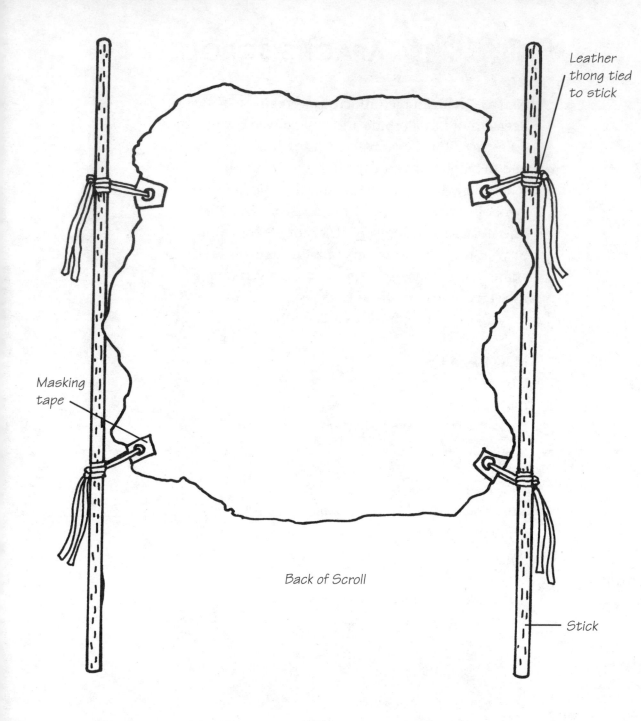

Leather
thong tied
to stick

Masking
tape

Back of Scroll

Stick

1. Use the scissors to cut the paper to about 24 inches square. Cut the edges unevenly, as shown, to make it look like an animal hide.

2. Decide which side will be the front of your scroll. On the back of the scroll, place a patch of masking tape at each of the four corners. Use the paper punch to make a hole at each corner, punching through the paper and the masking tape.

3. Cut the leather thongs in half (or cut twine into four 20-inch-long pieces). Run each of the four pieces through a corner hole, and tie them to the two sticks as shown.

4. Use the pencil to draw your story on the scroll, by using the pictures and symbols shown or creating your own. Mark lightly with the pencil so that you can erase mistakes. (Lighter pencil marks will also be better covered by the paint.)

5. Paint each of your pictures and symbols in whatever colors you choose. (Native Americans often used paints in imaginative ways. One Comanche scroll shows a green horse.) Use felt-tip pens to add tiny details.

6. When the scroll is finished, roll it up or hang it on the wall for decoration.

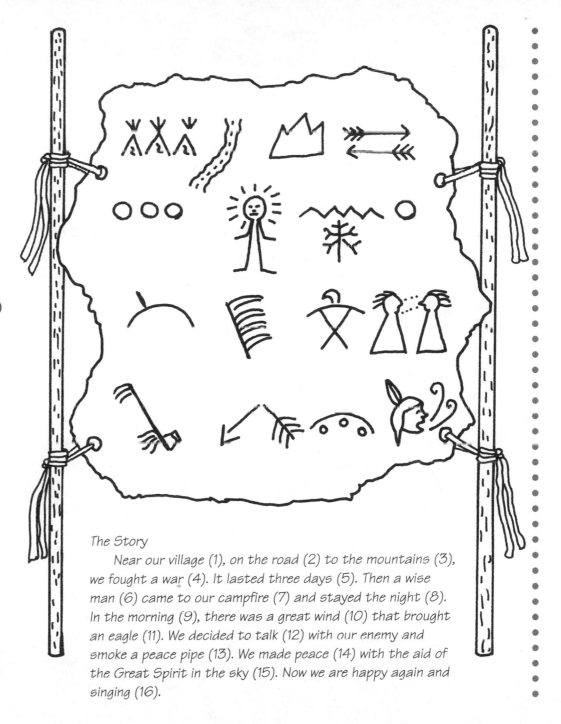

The Story

Near our village (1), on the road (2) to the mountains (3), we fought a war (4). It lasted three days (5). Then a wise man (6) came to our campfire (7) and stayed the night (8). In the morning (9), there was a great wind (10) that brought an eagle (11). We decided to talk (12) with our enemy and smoke a peace pipe (13). We made peace (14) with the aid of the Great Spirit in the sky (15). Now we are happy again and singing (16).

 **NAVAJO SANDPAINTING**

True Navajo sandpaintings were made to last only for the day. For some religious ceremonies, the Navajo made sandpaintings outdoors on a deerskin or a level area of sand, but more often they performed the work in the hogan, or house. Your sandpainting will be a permanent one that you can frame and hang on a wall. Instead of grinding plant and mineral materials into colored powders, you'll use powdered poster paints.

MATERIALS

several sheets of newspaper

pencil

9-by-12-inch tan poster board or white poster board with a base coat of light tan poster paint

ruler

powdered poster paints: red, yellow, blue (or turquoise), white, tan

several small paper plates

small pailful of clean sand (available at lumberyards and hardware stores)

several small scrap pieces of poster board

water

white glue

small paintbrush or toothpick

5-by-8-inch sheet of paper (optional)

1. Spread newspaper over your work surface.

2. Use the pencil to draw your design on the poster board. Either use the pattern shown, or invent your own. Use a ruler for straight lines.

3. Decide which colors you're going to use for each part of the painting. Lightly pencil in the name of each color on the poster board.

4. Put each color of poster paint in a separate paper plate. Add a little sand to each color and use a scrap piece of poster board to mix the sand into the powdered paint.

5. Add a small amount of water to the glue bottle and shake it well. (This will make the glue spread more evenly.)

6. Cover a small area to be colored with white glue. Squirt the glue directly from the bottle onto your drawing. For a large area, spread the glue with a scrap of poster board. For a very small area, use the paintbrush to apply a little glue. *Note: It is best to glue one small area at a time so that you can apply the paint-and-sand mixture before the glue dries.*

7. While the glue is wet, sprinkle the chosen color onto the glue. You may find it useful to make a small pouring spout by folding a sheet of paper into a funnel shape. This will give you a little more control over the sprinkling.

Art for a Day

Navajo sandpaintings were one part of a religious ceremony that may have lasted for several days. The paintings were made by specially trained Navajo called the singers. One singer created a painting to help heal an ailing person by restoring the balance between the human and the spiritual forces. At the same time, other singers repeated sacred chants and shook gourd rattles.

The long, thin figures in many of the sandpaintings represented the spirits. Other common sandpainting symbols were lightning and sacred plants, like corn and squash. At the end of the day, the singers carefully swept each color onto a piece of deerskin. Then they deposited the powders beneath trees to the north, south, east, and west. The next day, at dawn, they began a new painting.

8. Repeat steps 6 and 7 until all areas of the design have been colored.

9. Allow the glue to dry. Gently tap off any loose powder and sand that did not stick to the poster board. (If there are any bare spots on your painting, touch them up by using a small brush to apply a little poster paint mixed with water.)

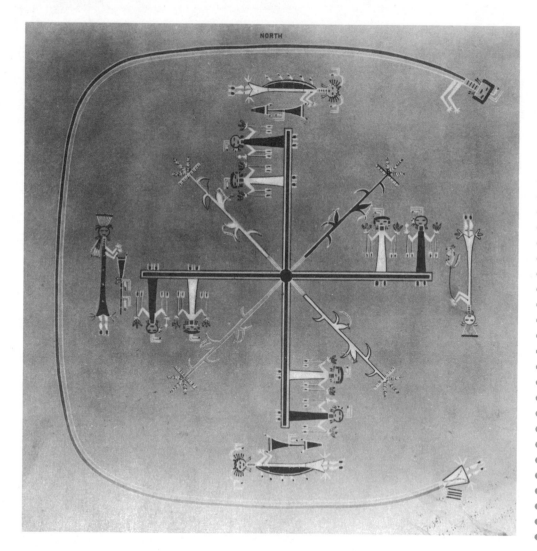

CHAPTER THREE

AUTUMN

PROJECTS

APPLE BUTTER

SPOON BREAD

ROASTED PUMPKIN
SEEDS

CORNHUSK DOLLS

HALLOWEEN
GHOSTS

TORTILLAS

THE MAGIC WALLET

WOOD CHOPPERS

CANADIAN GOOSE
WHIRLIGIG

The fair at Council Grove marked the end of the summer season and the beginning of the autumn harvest. The most urgent autumn job was bringing in the grain crops. Sam was proud that his father thought he was old enough to cut the wheat, even though he cut his hand several times on the curved blade of the sickle. After cutting, they raked the wheat and bound it. Next, with Liz and Mrs. Butler's help, they threshed the wheat on the floor of the barn by knocking the seeds loose with wooden flails. Finally, they winnowed the grain by tossing basketfuls in the air. The wind carried away the chaff, or seed husks, while the heavier golden grains fell back into the basket.

Next the Butler family harvested the vegetables. They stored the crops in a deep root cellar Mr. Butler and Sam dug and covered with a wooden frame and door.

AUTUMN DELIGHTS

Although the harvest demanded some of the hardest work of the year, it also brought many good things. Fresh-picked fruits and vegetables now replaced the dried, salted, and pickled foods that had carried them through the winter and part of the growing season. They now had plenty of food for the winter, with a good deal left over to sell or trade. They traded some of the surplus harvest in Council Grove in exchange for having their wheat milled into flour and some of the corn ground into cornmeal.

Liz and her mother used the first of the cornmeal for a family favorite of spoon bread. Throughout the autumn, the cabin was filled with the delicious smells of bread and pies baking in the oven built into the fireplace. When Mrs. Butler baked the year's first

pumpkin pies, she let Liz roast the pumpkin seeds for snacks.

The one crop the family missed was the apples from their New York farm. After the harvest, Sam and his father rode all the way to Missouri, where more settled farms had plenty of apples to sell or trade. Mr. Butler traded a side of beef for thirty bushels of apples. Mrs. Butler stored the apples, then used some of them to make another favorite recipe, apple butter.

 **APPLE BUTTER**

Here's a pioneer recipe for apple butter. Use the apple butter in place of butter or jam as a great spread for toast, English muffins, or plain bread. Your apple butter will stay fresh in the refrigerator for up to 2 weeks.

INGREDIENTS

4 cups applesauce

1 cup light brown sugar

¼ teaspoon each of cinnamon, ground cloves, and allspice

1 lemon

EQUIPMENT

mixing bowl

mixing spoon

grater

plastic wrap

baking dish

adult helper

MAKES

about sixteen 1-tablespoon servings

1. Preheat the oven to 275°F.

2. Put the applesauce, brown sugar, and spices in the mixing bowl. Stir well so that all the ingredients are blended.

Traveling Recipes

By the mid-1800s, each region of the country had its own special recipes. For example, New England became famous for dishes like clam chowder, baked beans, and brown bread. Maryland was known for its crab cakes, Louisiana for its jambalaya and Creole dishes, and Mexican Texas for spicy dishes like chili con carne.

In Pennsylvania, settlers from parts of Germany became known as Pennsylvania Dutch. (They weren't Dutch, but in the German language the word for German is Deutsch [doytch], which sounded like Dutch to other settlers.) The Pennsylvania Dutch became known for their folk arts and for their cooking. Since many wagon trains passed through Pennsylvania, westward-bound pioneers learned about these great recipes and carried them with them to the frontier. Apple butter was a favorite Pennsylvania Dutch recipe that made the journey west.

3. Have the adult help you grate the rind of half the lemon into the mixture. (Wrap the leftover lemon in plastic wrap and save for other uses.)

4. Spread the mixture into the baking dish.

5. Bake for about 3 hours. Every 15 to 20 minutes, have your adult helper pull the oven rack out so you can stir the apple butter mixture. When the mixture becomes very thick, it is done.

6. Have the adult remove the apple butter from the oven. Allow it to cool.

7. Serve by spreading the apple butter like jam on toast or English muffins. Refrigerate what you don't use.

PROJECT SPOON BREAD

Spoon bread was another favorite recipe of the pioneers, especially in the autumn. It was usually served warm as a side dish with chicken or roast beef. Once you've made the recipe, you'll know why they liked it so much—and why they called it spoon bread.

INGREDIENTS

5 tablespoons butter
1 cup milk
½ cup yellow cornmeal
½ teaspoon salt
3 eggs

EQUIPMENT

paper towel
2-quart baking dish or casserole
large saucepan
mixing spoon
large mixing bowl
spatula
small mixing bowl
eggbeater or wire whip
large serving spoon
adult helper

MAKES

5 to 6 servings

1. Preheat the oven to 375°F.

2. Use a paper towel and 1 tablespoon butter to lightly butter a baking dish.

3. Ask the adult to heat the milk in a saucepan without letting it boil.

4. Slowly sprinkle the cornmeal into the hot milk over medium heat, stirring constantly. Continue to cook and stir, without boiling, until the mixture is smooth and thick, liked cooked cereal.

5. Add the salt, then the rest of the butter, stirring until the butter is dissolved.

6. Remove the saucepan from the heat and transfer the mixture to a large mixing bowl. Use a spatula to scrape all of the mixture from the saucepan.

7. Ask the adult to help you crack the eggs and separate the whites from the yolks. Drip the whites into a small mixing bowl, and add the yolks directly to the batter in the large bowl.

Corn or Wheat?

With the opening of the Erie Canal in 1825, Western farmers had an inexpensive way to ship their products to the growing cities of the East. They soon learned that people in the cities liked wheat bread better than cornmeal products. By the 1840s, Americans were eating more wheat than corn for the first time in their history.

No matter how important wheat became, however, pioneer farmers knew they still had to grow a great deal of corn. Three or four acres of field corn provided a full year's feed for a family's livestock. People used corn for oil, starch, syrup, and in relish. It could be used in hot breakfast cereal, chowders and stews, or as an occasional treat— popcorn or roasted corn on the cob.

8. Beat the egg whites in the small bowl until they are stiff but not dry.

9. Mix the whites into the cornmeal batter a little at a time. Use the spatula to fold the whites in rather than stir.

10. Pour the batter into the lightly buttered baking dish. Smooth the top with the spoon or spatula.

11. Bake for 35 to 40 minutes, until the top is golden brown. Have the adult remove the dish from the oven.

12. Serve the spoon bread warm, using a large serving spoon.

 **ROASTED PUMPKIN SEEDS**

When your family carves a Halloween pumpkin, save the seeds for roasting. Salted or plain, they make a delicious, chewy snack food, and one that is high in nutrition. Cleaning the seeds is messy work, but the results are worth it.

INGREDIENTS
pumpkin
tap water
2 tablespoons vegetable oil or shortening
½ teaspoon salt

EQUIPMENT
carving knife (to be handled only by an adult)
large metal spoon
colander
paper towels
cookie sheet
plastic or tin container with lid
adult helper

MAKES
4 to 6 snack servings

1. Have the adult cut open the pumpkin. Scrape out the seeds with a large spoon and place them in a colander. Remove as much of the pumpkin fiber as you can as you scoop out the seeds.

2. Place the colander under cool running water and clean the seeds with your fingers. (Don't worry if some of the fiber remains stuck to the seeds. After roasting, it dries and is easier to remove.) Place the seeds on paper towels to dry.

3. Preheat the oven to 275°F.

4. Use a paper towel to lightly oil the cookie sheet. Spread the seeds on the oiled cookie sheet.

5. Sprinkle salt over the seeds and bake for about 45 minutes. Have the adult shake the cookie sheet every few minutes.

6. Turn up the heat to 350°F for 5 minutes. The seeds should become lightly browned. When the seeds start to darken, they are done.

7. Have the adult remove the cookie sheet from the oven. Allow the seeds to cool.

8. Eat some seeds warm and store the rest in a container with a lid. The roasted seeds will stay fresh for several weeks.

HARVEST DECORATIONS

During the harvest, Sam and his father picked the corn as soon as the ears were ripe. A little of the corn was used right away, but they stored most of it in the barn until the other harvest work was finished. They cut up the stalks for feeding the livestock, but removing the husks from the corn was one of the last autumn tasks. The Butlers joined with neighboring settlers to hold a cornhusking bee. Cornhusking bees were already a tradition in American farm communities.

Husking corn was not hard work, but it took a lot of time. Turning the chore into a party made the work go faster, and it was a good excuse for pioneer families to get together before the long winter. The settlers divided into two teams and had a contest to see which team could produce the largest pile of ears. The work was followed by a huge harvest feast.

Mrs. Butler showed the children another harvest tradition by using some of the cornhusks to create harvest dolls. Harvest dolls were for decoration and good luck, rather than for play. Liz and her mother found other ways to decorate the cabin for the harvest season. They made arrangements of brightly colored leaves and dried grasses, and placed baskets of apples and nuts on the table and cupboard.

PROJECT CORNHUSK DOLLS

Cornhusk dolls are still made today and used for table decorations, especially during the Thanksgiving season. Work with a friend to make several of these harvest figures. You can also use small pieces as autumn decorations, by adding them to a basket, a rake, or even a turkey.

Cornhusks have a smooth side and a rough side. In this project, be sure to always keep the smooth side facing out.

MATERIALS

8 to 10 large pieces of cornhusk (Remove from fresh corn or purchase dried husks from a crafts store, produce stand, or supermarket.)

several sheets of newspaper

pan of tap water

timer

damp towel or rag

scissors

5 to 7 cotton balls

heavy thread (tan or beige) or twine

ruler

6-inch piece of flexible wire or a pipe cleaner

white glue or craft glue

corn silk

black and red fine-point felt-tip pens

1. If the cornhusks are green, dry them until they are straw-colored. Do this by placing them between sheets of newspaper. Store in a warm, dry place for 5 or 6 days, or until the color turns.

2. Cover your work area with more newspaper. Soak the dried husks in the pan of water for about 5 minutes before you begin working with them. This will make them softer and easier to shape.

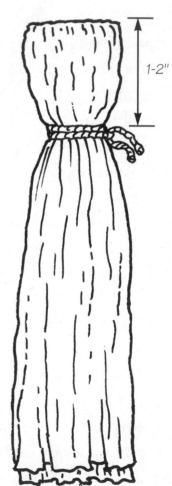

1-2"

3. Remove all the husks from the water and shake the water out of them. Cover the ones you are not working with, with a damp towel.

4. Cut off the pointed tips of all the husks to make the shapes more alike.

5. Form the doll's head by taking a large piece of husk and folding it in half. Stuff 3 or 4 cotton balls under the fold. Tie a piece of heavy thread around the husk 1 to 2 inches from the fold to create a head shape. The ends of the husks will extend several inches below the neck.

6. For the arms, cut a thin piece of husk about 7 inches long and wrap it around the 6-inch piece of wire. Fold back the tips of the husk at each end

of the wire. Tie them with the thread at the wrists to form hands.

7. Slide the husk-covered wire between the two halves of the husk below the figure's head to form the arms, one on each side of the body. Carefully bend the arms into any position you wish.

8. Tie a piece of thread around the doll's waist. Stuff 2 or 3 cotton balls between the husks to fill out the torso.

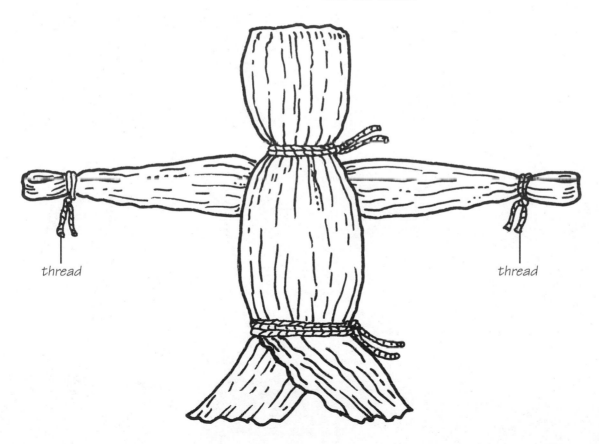

thread   thread

9. For a full skirt, place 3 or 4 husks around the doll's waist, but point the husks up, so that they extend above the figure's head. Tie the husks around the waist with thread, then fold them down over the tied thread to create the skirt.

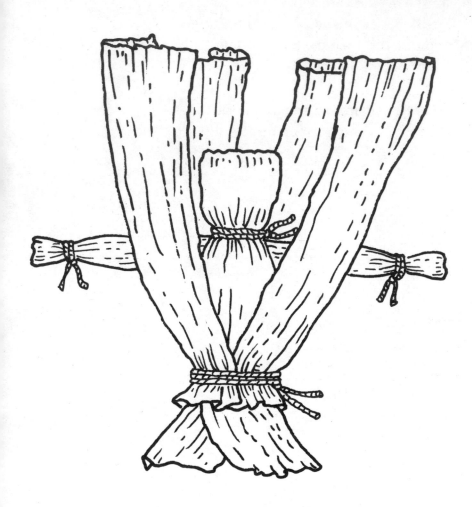

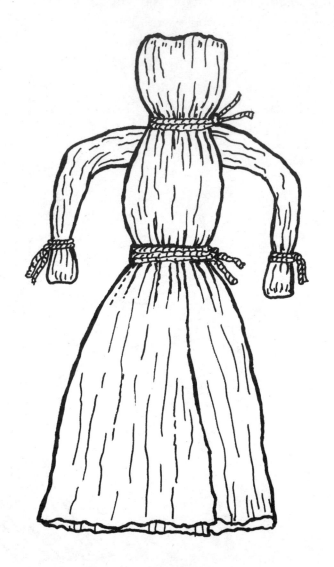

10. Glue a little corn silk to the head for hair.

11. Use felt-tip pens to add facial features—eyes, eyebrows, nose, and mouth.

 **HALLOWEEN GHOSTS**

Some of the easiest autumn decorations to make are little white ghosts for Halloween. Make a few to hang in windows, or from bushes, trees, and porches. You can make them as big as you want.

MATERIALS
scissors
ruler
old white sheet or pillowcase (Be sure to ask adult
*   permission before using.)*
2 to 3 sheets of newspaper
string
paper clip
black marker

1. Cut a 16-inch square from the old sheet.

2. Crumple the sheets of newspaper into a tight ball. Wrap the square cloth around the ball.

3. Cut a piece of string about 6 inches long and tie it below the ball of newspaper to form the neck and head.

4. Unbend the paper clip in the middle so that it forms a long S. Push one end of the paper clip through the cloth at the top of the head.

Imported from Ireland

Halloween was brought to the United States by Irish immigrants in the 1830s. In ancient times, the Irish and Scots had celebrated the eve of the new year on October 31. It was a time for building huge bonfires on the hills to frighten away evil spirits. They also believed that on that night, the spirits of the dead came back to visit their homes, while witches, hobgoblins, and black cats roamed the darkness.

When Christianity came to Ireland and Scotland, these ancient beliefs became mixed with the Christian celebration on the eve of All Saints' Day or All Hallows' Day. All Hallow Eve was also on October 31. The Irish also had a tradition of carving a face on a turnip. When Irish immigrants came to America, they found that carving a pumpkin was even better than carving a turnip.

5. Cut a piece of string 8 to 10 inches long and tie it to the upper end of the paper clip to make a loop for hanging.

6. Draw large round eyes on the head with the marker.

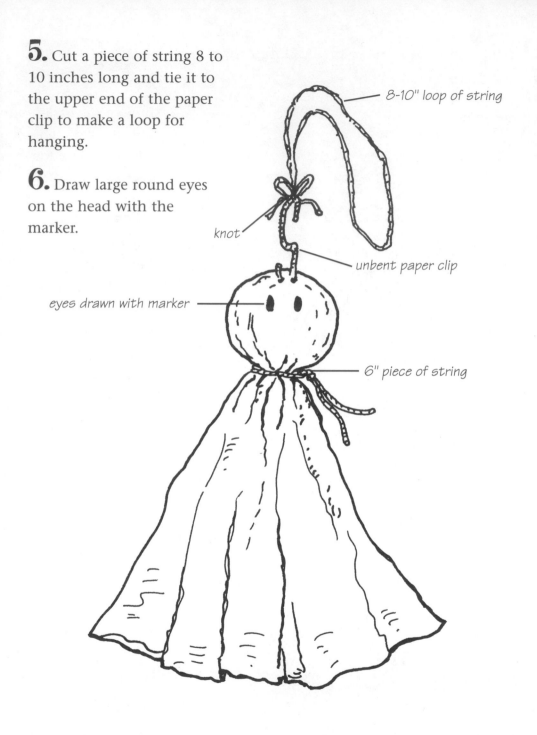

8-10" loop of string

knot

unbent paper clip

eyes drawn with marker

6" piece of string

TREASURES FROM THE SOUTHWEST

When the last crops had been stored, and the meat was salted and smoked, the Butlers made a trading trip to Council Grove. At the general store, Mr. Butler traded some of their extra grain and meat for things they would need over the winter, like salt, sugar, and lemons.

While they were in town, a long wagon train rumbled into the settlement from the Santa Fe Trail. Liz and Sam counted twenty-six wagons, each loaded with trade goods from the Southwest. One of the wagon masters gave Mrs. Butler new recipes, including one for tortillas.

PROJECT TORTILLAS

Tortillas (tor-TEE-yuhs) are easy—and fun—to make. You can eat them warm with butter, or use them to make tacos, enchiladas, or burritos. The main ingredient is corn flour, called masa harina, which is available at most supermarkets.

INGREDIENTS
2¼ cups masa harina (corn flour)
1 teaspoon salt
1½ cups warm tap water
1 tablespoon flour
shortening

EQUIPMENT
mixing spoon
mixing bowl
pastry board
2 sheets of waxed paper
rolling pin
ruler
pancake griddle or skillet
pancake turner
towel or aluminum foil
adult helper

MAKES
12 tortillas

1. Mix the masa harina and salt in a mixing bowl.

2. Stir in 1 cup of water, a little at a time. Stir constantly to keep lumps from forming. Beat the mixture thoroughly with the spoon.

3. Sprinkle the flour evenly over the pastry board. Place the dough on the lightly floured pastry board and knead it. To knead the dough, push it forward with the heels of your hands, then pull it back. Sprinkle a little of the remaining water on the dough as needed. Continue kneading and adding water until the dough is smooth and firm enough that it does not stick to your fingers.

4. Divide the dough into 12 equal pieces. Form each piece into a round ball.

5. Spread a little shortening on both sheets of waxed paper. Lay one sheet on the pastry board and place the 12 dough balls on the sheet. Allow plenty of space between each ball. Cover with the second sheet of waxed paper.

6. Use the rolling pin to press and roll the balls until they are flat and very thin. Each tortilla should be about 5 inches in diameter.

7. Ask the adult to heat the griddle (ungreased) over moderate heat, and cook the tortillas one at a time. Allow $1\frac{1}{2}$ to 2 minutes on each side. Turn once with the pancake turner.

8. As the tortillas are cooked, stack them, and wrap them in a clean towel. (They can also be reheated in the oven at low heat.)

9. Serve them plain or in your favorite Tex-Mex recipe.

TIME FOR TOYS

On the trip back to Cotters Creek, the Butlers were stopped by a fierce autumn storm. The wagon got stuck in mud and they were forced to spend a cold, wet night huddled under a piece of canvas. When they finally reached home the next day, they were thankful for the comfort the cabin provided.

The storm that struck the Butlers on their way home from Council Grove left both Liz and Sam with heavy colds. Their mother roasted lemons in front of the fire, then mixed the juice with honey, rosemary, and comfrey root. The medicine eased Liz's and Sam's sore throats, but they had to stay in the cabin for several days and sleep on the floor in front of the fireplace.

While the children were recovering, their parents helped them catch up on their lessons in reading, writing, and numbers. Their father also showed them how to make some new toys. Liz and Sam thought that making the toys was as much fun as

playing with them. They were especially fascinated by any toy that moved, so all of the toys Mr. Butler helped them with involved some form of motion. They used wood scraps to make a pair of wood choppers and a toy called a whirligig that moved in the wind, like a miniature windmill. And Mr. Butler used blocks of wood to make a toy called a magic wallet.

PROJECT THE MAGIC WALLET

The magic wallet is a simple trick toy that was popular throughout the 1800s. It's easy to make, and it's fun to figure out how it works.

MATERIALS

scissors
ruler
about 30 inches of ¼- or ⅜-inch-wide cloth ribbon,
  any color
8 flat-head thumbtacks
2 flat blocks of wood, about 7 inches long and 3¾
  inches wide (Note: If blocks have rough edges, have
  an adult use sandpaper to smooth them.)
hammer (to be used only by an adult)
dollar bill
adult helper

1. Cut the ribbon into 4 pieces, each 7½ inches long.

2. Fold under the ends of 2 ribbons about ¼ inch, and thumbtack them to the long end of one block as shown. If the thumbtacks will not go all the way in, ask an adult to hammer them.

3. Fold under the ends of the other 2 ribbons, and tack them to the other end of the same block. Crisscross them over the block as shown.

4. Place the second block over the first, as shown, with the 4 ribbons in between the blocks. Pull the crisscrossed ribbons tight, fold under the ends ¼ inch, and tack them to one end of the top block. Tack the other 2, parallel ribbons to the other end of the top block. Cut off any extra ribbon.

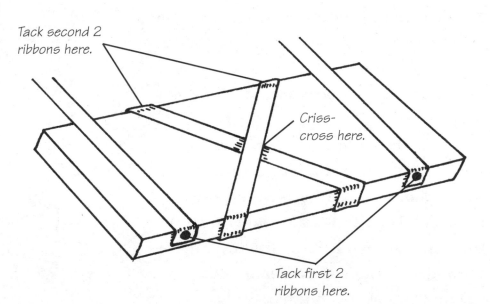

Tack second 2 ribbons here.

Criss-cross here.

Tack first 2 ribbons here.

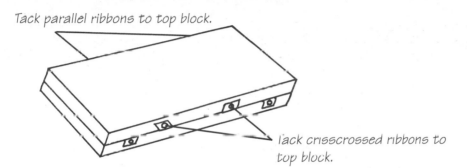

Tack parallel ribbons to top block.

Tack crisscrossed ribbons to top block.

5. Open the magic wallet. Place a dollar bill under the parallel ribbons. Close the wallet, then open it in the other direction. Presto! The dollar bill has magically moved to the other side.

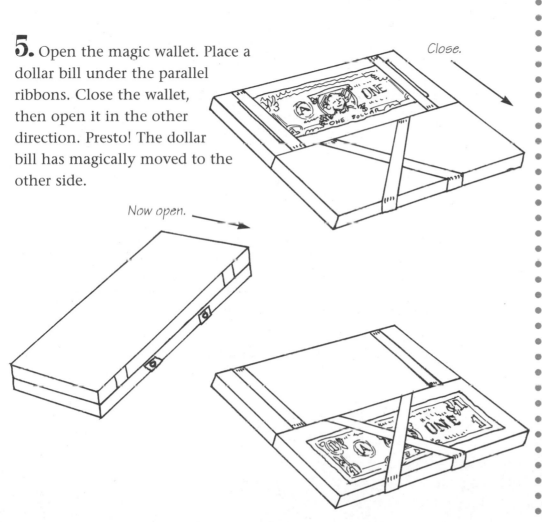

Close.

Now open.

Frontier Medicine

In the 1840s, the number of trained doctors in the United States was growing rapidly, but few had yet moved to the frontier. Even where doctors were available, pioneer families usually relied more on medicines made from herbs, roots, and barks. These folk remedies were often as helpful as anything doctors could do at that time. It would be another thirty years before scientists learned that germs and viruses cause disease. Medical treatments improved rapidly after that.

This project is based on a toy first created in Switzerland and Germany. The toys became popular in the United States in the early 1800s and were sometimes made by professional wood-carvers. While pioneer kids and wood-carvers made the toy out of nails and thin pieces of wood, you can create the same thing with poster board, craft sticks, and paper fasteners. You can even make different kinds of bobbing toys, such as two women kneading dough, two blacksmiths pounding on an anvil, or your own creation.

MATERIALS

white poster board
pencil
scissors
one-hole paper punch
crayons or colored markers
black felt-tip fine-point pen
2 craft sticks
awl or compass point (to be used only by an adult)
4 short brass paper fasteners
white glue
adult helper

1. On the poster board, copy the drawings of the log and the 2 men on page 77, including the arms and axes. Carefully cut out the 3 pieces.

2. Use the paper punch to make two holes in the leg and foot of each man as shown.

3. Color the men and log with crayons, using whichever colors you wish. Add facial features and any other details with felt-tip pen.

4. Line up the 2 men and the craft sticks as shown. Ask your adult helper to use the awl to make two holes in each stick to line up with the two holes in the leg and foot of each man. Make one hole about ½ inch from the end of the stick and the second hole about 2 inches from the other end of the stick. The holes in the sticks must be large enough for the paper fasteners to fit through.

5. Push a paper fastener through the foot of each man and through the holes of one craft stick. Push the other 2 fasteners through the leg of each man and through the holes of the other craft stick. Bend back the prongs of the fasteners.

6. Glue the log to the upper craft stick in between the 2 men as shown.

7. Using the ends of the craft sticks as handles, hold one handle steady and pull the other. As you pull each handle, and then push it back, the men will take turns chopping the log.

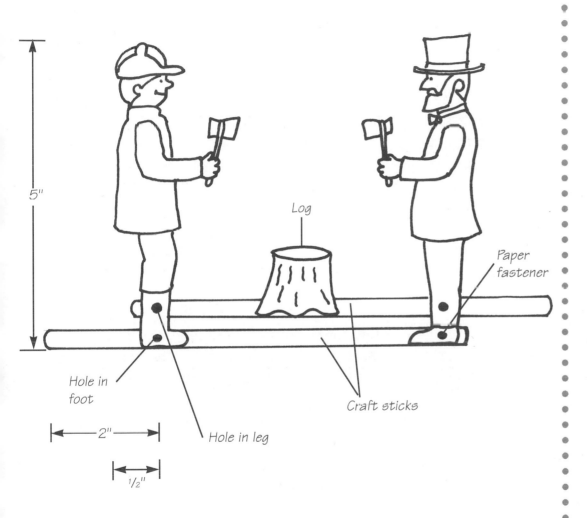

5"

Log

Paper fastener

Hole in foot

Craft sticks

2"

Hole in leg

1/2"

Until the 1830s, most kids' toys were made of wood. Wooden toys that moved, like wood choppers and whirligigs, were very popular. Then, in the early 1830s, tin became more plentiful, and toy makers began making windup toys out of tin. The tin was flimsy, but kids loved the steam engines that moved and figures that danced on the top of a box. The springs used to wind up the toys broke easily, so the tin toys didn't last nearly as long as those made of wood.

PROJECT • CANADIAN GOOSE WHIRLIGIG

Whirligigs are something like miniature weather vanes, which are used to show the direction the wind is blowing. Whirligigs are small wooden figures of people or animals, with paddlelike arms or wings that turn in the wind. The faster the wind blows, the faster the paddles whirl. No one knows whether the first whirligigs were made to be weather vanes or as toys for kids. But both kids and adults enjoyed them and often stuck them on fence posts.

Instead of making your whirligig by carving wood, you can use poster board or cardboard. The result will look much like the whirligigs pioneer kids made, and will also show you how fast the wind is blowing.

MATERIALS

pencil
white poster board or cardboard
ruler
scissors
crayons or markers
fine-point brown marker or colored pencil (optional)
awl or compass point (to be used only by an adult)
¼-inch dowel or ¼-inch-wide scrap of wood about 1 inch long
white glue
2 brads about ½ inch long
hammer
flat piece of wood, about ½ inch wide and 12 inches long (An old ruler will work.)
adult helper

1. Use the pencil to copy the pattern for the goose and wing on page 79 onto the poster board. The goose should measure about 8 inches from beak to tail, and the wing should be about 6 inches long. Both pieces should be about 3 inches wide.

2. Cut out the 2 pieces. Outline the wing on another piece of poster board and cut out a second wing.

3. Color the goose according to the color scheme. Use brown to make featherlike markings on the body and wings.

4. Have an adult use the awl to make a hole in the body, just large enough for the dowel to fit through. Make a small hole in each wing large enough for the brads to fit through easily.

5. Push the dowel through the hole in the body so that the dowel fits snugly in the hole. About ½ inch of the dowel will be on either side of the

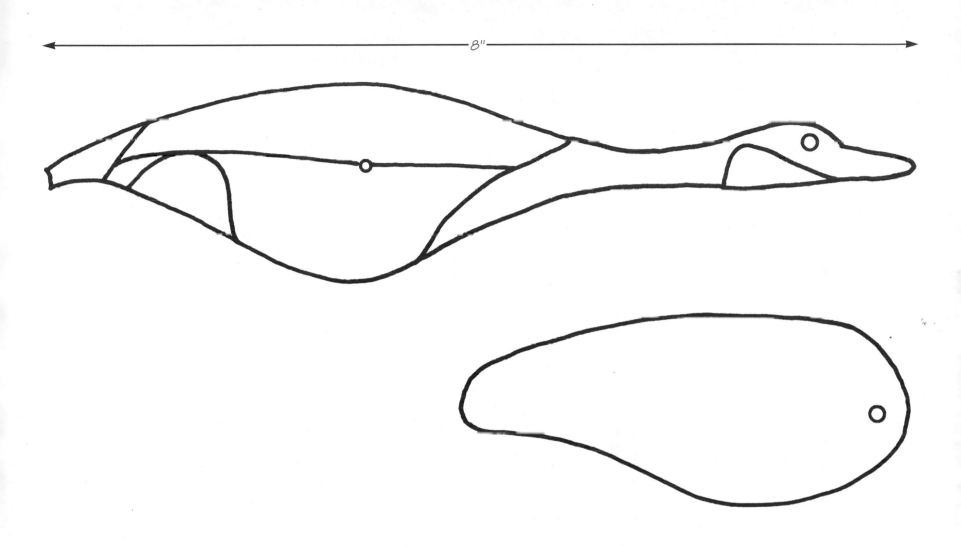

8"

body. Put a few drops of glue on the middle of the dowel to help fix it in place. Allow the glue to dry.

6. Place a brad in each wing hole so that the wing can turn freely on the brad.

7. Ask the adult to use the hammer to attach each wing to the dowel by tapping the brads into each end of the dowel. The brads should be hammered in loosely so that the wings will spin.

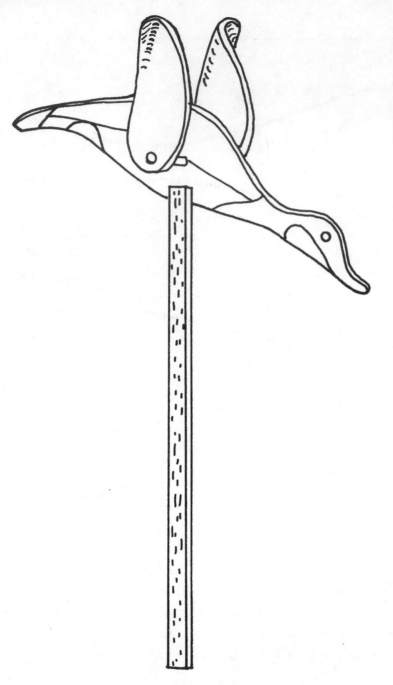

8. Grip the top of each wing with your fingers and bend it torward the goose's head so that it can catch the wind.

9. Glue the body to the piece of wood. Allow the glue to dry.

10. Take your whirligig outdoors and hold it up in the breeze. The wings will spin fast or slow, depending on the speed of the wind.

CHAPTER FOUR

WINTER

PINECONE ANGEL

SALT DOUGH
ORNAMENTS

OJO DE DIOS

SILHOUETTE
PORTRAIT

PICTURE FRAME

SEMINOLE
PATCHWORK

LEAF-PRINT
WRAPPING PAPER

TANGRAM

FOLK ART
CHECKERBOARD
AND GAME

BEANBAG TARGET
GAME

Winter brought more changes to life on the Butler homestead. Grain, vegetables, fruits, and meat had all been safely stored in the root cellar. The family could look back on their first full year at Cotters Creek with satisfaction and hope for an even better year in 1844.

There was plenty of work to do over the winter months, but the pace was more relaxed. Sam helped his father chop firewood. They plastered chinks in the cabin timbers and repaired roof shingles. They continued to tend to the livestock every day, repaired and cleaned tools, and worked on finishing the barn. For Liz and her mother, the daily routine of baking, preparing meals, and sewing or weaving was not much different from the other seasons of the year. But now the family had longer evenings together to work on crafts, play games, read, and continue Liz's and Sam's lessons.

HOLIDAY PREPARATIONS

By early December, the Butlers were satisfied that their cabin was snug and comfortable for the winter. Now it was time to prepare for the holidays. First came Thanksgiving during the first week in December. Thanksgiving was not a national holiday in 1843, but most Americans celebrated it with a feast and a church service. The Butlers planned to travel four miles to the Taylors' to lead a prayer service there for several families.

The family also celebrated Christmas. They did not plan to have a Christmas tree, but everyone in the family pitched in to decorate the cabin with pine boughs, wreaths, and handmade ornaments that they hung in the windows and from the heavy beams. They made ornaments out of salt dough, and a yarn decoration called ojo de Dios. The children added wings and faces to pinecones to make angel table decorations.

PROJECT PINECONE ANGEL

Pioneer families used different kinds of berries, nuts, and pine cones to make ornaments and table decorations. Pinecones and nuts can be formed into all kinds of shapes—animals, people, and, in this project, an angel. You can use your pinecone angel as a table decoration.

MATERIALS

pinecone, 3 to 4 inches high
tap water
pencil
white lightweight poster board or cardboard
ruler
scissors
white glue
small round nut, such as a hickory nut
black fine-point felt-tip pen

1. Choose a pinecone that stands up straight when you set it on its base. Sprinkle water on the cone. This will close up the petals of the pinecone, making it easier to work with.

2. Use the pencil to copy the wings in the drawing on page 84 onto the poster board. The wings should be approximately 2 inches wide and 3 inches long.

3. Cut out the wings and glue them to the pinecone. You may need to use the scissors to cut off 1 or 2 petals to create a flat enough surface for gluing the wings.

The Arrival of Christmas

The celebration of Christmas with decorations and gifts did not develop in the United States until the 1820s and 1830s. According to legend, the idea of a decorated Christmas tree was introduced by German soldiers who had been hired to fight for the British during the American Revolution.

The tree did not become part of the American holiday tradition until about 1830. In 1822, a man named Clement C. Moore wrote the poem that begins "'Twas the night before Christmas." The poem helped make Christmas a much more popular holiday. By 1843, Christmas was beginning to look like the festive holiday we know—a time for family gatherings, a traditional dinner, decorations, and, of course, gifts.

4. Use the scissors to cut off the top petals of the cone so that the nut will sit firmly on the top of the cone. Glue the nut to the top of the cone for the head.

5. Add facial features to the nut with felt-tip pen.

6. Cut a small, thin circle of poster board for a halo. Glue it near the top of the head.

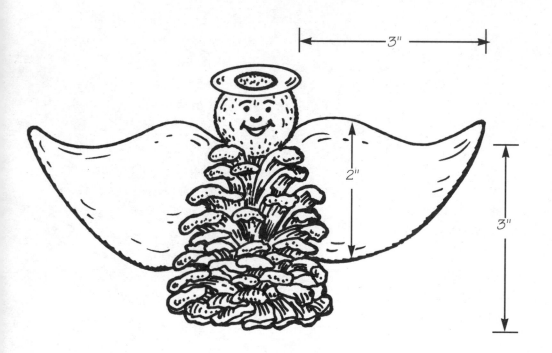

PROJECT **SALT DOUGH ORNAMENTS**

One of the most common ways of making ornaments in the pioneer times was to shape them out of dough. With a batch of special salt dough and some acrylic paints, you can make some wonderful decorations for Christmas or any other celebration.

Recipes for salt dough vary a great deal. Once you begin to knead the dough, you can add a little more water, or a little more flour, to make a dough that feels almost like soft modeling clay. *(Note: Do not eat the dough.)*

MATERIALS
2½ cups flour
1 cup salt
large mixing bowl
mixing spoon
1½ cups water
pastry board
timer
rolling pin
ruler
cookie cutters
knitting needle
paper towel
1 tablespoon cooking oil
1 or 2 cookie sheets
small paintbrush

acrylic paints or poster paints: any colors
scissors
scraps of yarn: red, green, or other colors
waxed paper or sandwich bags
shoe box or other sturdy box
adult helper

1. Combine 2 cups of flour and the salt in a large mixing bowl.

2. Use the mixing spoon to slowly stir in about 1½ cups of water, a little at a time. As the dough becomes thicker, use your hands to mix.

3. Sprinkle a little of the remaining flour on a pastry board and place the dough on it. Knead the dough for 5 to 10 minutes, or until it feels like modeling clay. Add a little flour, or a little water, if necessary.

4. Roll out the dough with a rolling pin until it is about ¼ inch thick. (Don't make it any thicker, as thicker dough takes much longer to bake.)

5. Cut shapes out of the dough with cookie cutters. Scrape together the scraps of leftover dough, form it into a ball, and roll out the dough to cut a few more shapes. Save some dough for decorations and details.

6. Use scraps of dough to add details to your ornaments, such as Santa's nose and whiskers, or decorations on a stocking or wreath. As you shape these details, dab them with a little water to bond them to the ornament.

7. Use the knitting needle to make a hole in the top of each ornament for hanging.

Warning: Lighted Christmas Tree

Although most pioneer families did not have Christmas trees, by the late 1830s, many American families in towns and cities decorated trees as part of their Christmas celebration. They trimmed the tree on Christmas Eve, and everyone in the family took part. People stretched strings of popcorn, cranberries, and nuts around the tree, and carefully hung ornaments.

Some families decorated with candles as well. The lighting of the candles was a special moment, with everyone gathered around the tree. But the candles remained lit for only a few minutes. During that time, several of the men stood by with buckets of water, just in case!

8. Preheat the oven to 300°F. Use a paper towel to spread cooking oil very lightly on a cookie sheet, and place the ornaments on it. Space the ornaments so they are not touching each other.

9. Ask an adult to put the sheet in the oven to bake for about 1 hour. (If you have made many small ornaments, you may need a second cookie sheet.) Have the adult check for doneness: the

finished ornaments should be very hard, almost like clay that has hardened or been fired.

10. Have the adult remove the sheet from the oven. Allow the ornaments to dry thoroughly.

11. Decorate the ornaments with paints. Make sure to paint all parts of the ornament, including the back. This will seal the ornaments against moisture so they will last for several years.

12. Tie a 6-inch piece of yarn through the hole in each ornament for hanging. Store the ornaments by wrapping each one individually in waxed paper. Pack them lightly in the shoe box.

Salt Dough Ornaments

6" yarn

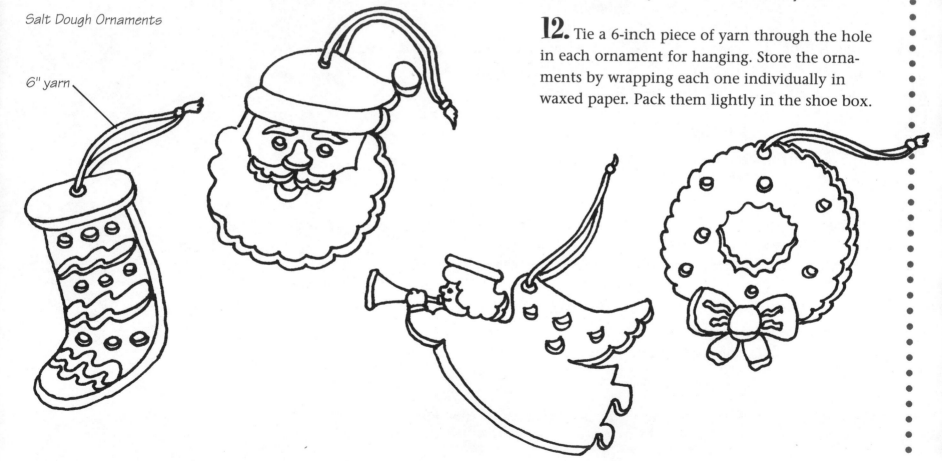

PROJECT OJO DE DIOS

The ojo de Dios (O-ho day DEE-ohs) is a good-luck decoration that was made by Hispanic settlers in the hills around Santa Fe in present-day New Mexico. These colorful decorations are still made by the descendants of those early settlers and also by people in Mexico. The ojo de Dios, which means "eye of God" in Spanish, was traditionally made for an October festival. But it also makes an attractive decoration for Christmas and the New Year. Hang your ojo on the wall, or use it as a tree decoration.

MATERIALS

two ¼-inch dowels or straight sticks, 10 to 12 inches long
scissors
yarn in 4 or 5 different colors
ruler

1. Make a square cross with the 2 dowels.

2. Cut a piece of yarn about 12 inches long. Tie one end of the yarn to one of the crosspieces, then wind it around the center. Wind the yarn tightly around the crossing point several times. This will bind the crosspieces together and form a bit of a lump, two or three strands thick. This lump will be the ojo, or "eye."

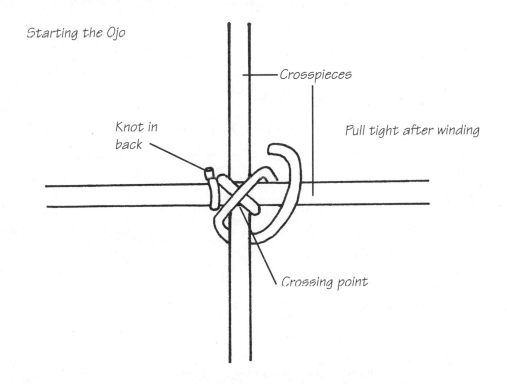

Starting the Ojo

Crosspieces

Knot in back

Pull tight after winding

Crossing point

3. Choose a second yarn color and tie the end of it to the end of the first piece of yarn. Try to make the knot close to a crosspiece. That way you can tuck the knot behind the crosspiece so that it doesn't show. Don't cut the second yarn color.

4. Wind the second color around a crosspiece one complete turn, then take it to the next crosspiece. Wind it once around that, and continue all the way around.

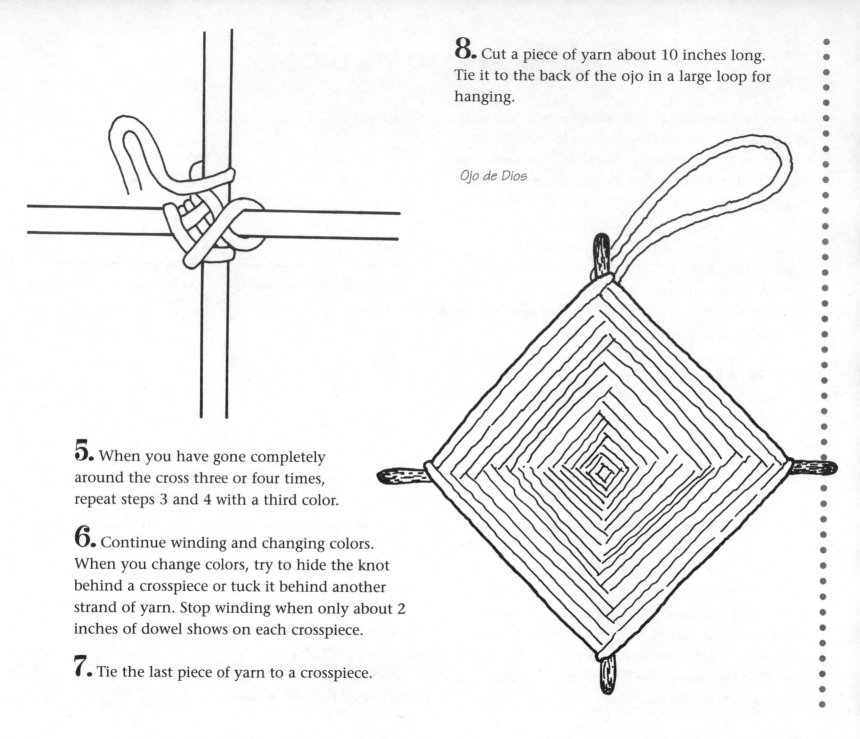

8. Cut a piece of yarn about 10 inches long. Tie it to the back of the ojo in a large loop for hanging.

Ojo de Dios

5. When you have gone completely around the cross three or four times, repeat steps 3 and 4 with a third color.

6. Continue winding and changing colors. When you change colors, try to hide the knot behind a crosspiece or tuck it behind another strand of yarn. Stop winding when only about 2 inches of dowel shows on each crosspiece.

7. Tie the last piece of yarn to a crosspiece.

HOLIDAY GIFTS

Liz and Sam enjoyed the holiday preparations, but they found that keeping secrets in the small cabin was difficult. They wanted to make silhouette portraits of themselves as a present for their mother, but the best light to use was the afternoon light in the main room of the cabin, where the entire family gathered.

The children did manage to keep the finished silhouettes out of sight, and they even were able to make special frames for their portraits. As a present for their father, Liz and Sam wanted to copy a design called Seminole patchwork. They had seen a Seminole chief in Council Grove wearing a color patchwork cloak. Liz knew it would take months to sew a cloak, or even a vest, in Seminole patchwork, so they decided to make a patchwork book cover for Mr. Butler.

Their mother showed Liz and Sam how to make wrapping paper

for their gifts. They used leaves to print designs on the brown and blue wrapping paper from the general store, and wrapped their presents in the homemade paper. Mr. Butler was delighted with his Seminole patchwork book cover, and Mrs. Butler proudly displayed the framed silhouette portraits of her children in the main room of the cabin.

Portraits in 1843

In the early 1800s, only people who were fairly wealthy could afford to have their portraits painted. Silhouettes were a popular substitute for true portraits. Viewers could easily identify the person, and the cost was very low.

In the late 1830s, a French artist named Louis Daguerre developed a technique for taking the first true photographs, called daguerrotypes. The technology of photography developed rapidly after that, and by the 1860s, photograph portraits were widely popular.

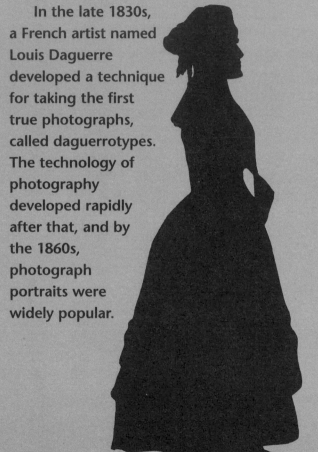

PROJECT SILHOUETTE PORTRAIT

A silhouette is a portrait cut from dark material and mounted on a light background. To create a silhouette, you'll need a partner and a bright, direct light. A floodlight or spotlight is ideal, but you can use any light that has a direct beam, such as a desk lamp or even a powerful flashlight.

MATERIALS

straight-back chair
blank wall for backdrop
bright light (spotlight, desk lamp, or flashlight)
2 sheets of white typing paper
masking tape
pencil
scissors
sheet of black construction paper
white glue
helper

1. Place the chair close to the wall. Have your partner sit in a comfortable position, with her side next to the wall.

2. Position the light to shine on your partner. Darken the room and adjust the light so that the shadow cast by the light makes a sharp profile on the wall.

3. Position a sheet of white paper on the wall so that the profile is now on the paper. Tape the paper in place. (Experiment a little until the light is right and the profile is the size you want.)

4. Have your partner remain perfectly still. With pencil, carefully trace the outline of her shadow on the white paper.

5. Cut out the profile, then tape it to the sheet of black construction paper.

Silhouette Portrait

6. Trace around the profile with pencil and cut out the black silhouette.

7. Center the black silhouette on the second sheet of white paper, then glue the silhouette to the paper. Make a frame for your silhouette in the next project.

PROJECT PICTURE FRAME

Pioneers made picture frames out of scraps of wood or molding. If the right pieces of wood were not available, they painted what looked like a frame around the edges of the painting. You can make a frame for your silhouette out of strips of poster board and cardboard. The directions are for a silhouette on an 8-by-10-inch sheet of paper. If your silhouette is smaller or larger, adjust the dimensions so that the frame makes a 2-inch border around the picture.

MATERIALS

several sheets of newspaper
ruler
pencil
stiff cardboard
scissors
black or dark brown poster board (If you only have white poster board, apply a coat of black poster paint or acrylic paint.)
white glue
silhouette from the previous project

1. Cover your work area with newspaper. Use ruler and pencil to mark a 12-by-14-inch rectangle on the cardboard. Cut out the rectangle with scissors.

2. With pencil and ruler, measure and mark 2 strips on the poster board, 2 inches wide and 10 inches long.

3. Mark 2 more strips, 2 inches wide and 12 inches long. Cut out the 4 strips.

4. Glue your silhouette to the center of the cardboard rectangle.

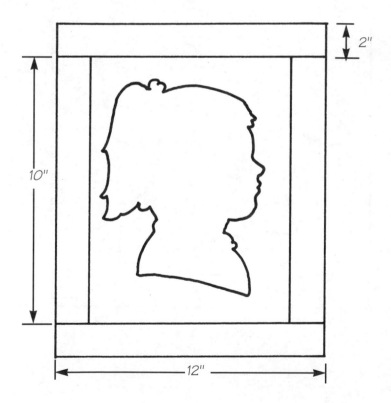

5. Glue the two 12-inch strips of poster board to the top and bottom of the cardboard as shown.

6. Glue the two 10-inch strips of poster board to the sides of the cardboard, as shown.

7. Measure and cut a 2-by-8-inch piece of cardboard to make a stand for the frame. Fold the cardboard 2 inches from one end.

8. Place the stand on the back of the frame as shown. Experiment with the position so that the stand allows the frame to stand upright. Glue the stand to the back of the frame.

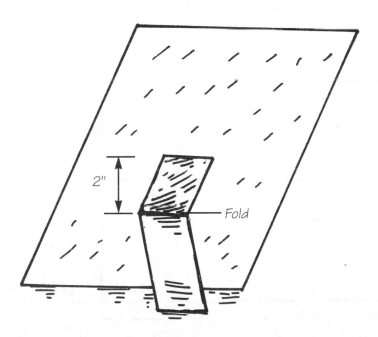

SEMINOLE PATCHWORK

Seminole patchwork is made by cutting and sewing narrow strips of fabric into bands. The bands are used to decorate clothing, like a shirt or dress. You'll make your bands with construction paper.

The finished band makes an attractive cover for a notebook, diary, or journal to give as a gift. The directions are for a band about 3½ inches wide and 6½ inches long. You can easily adjust the length or width for larger or smaller book covers.

MATERIALS

pencil
ruler
3 sheets of construction paper; any 3 colors that go
  well together
scissors
white glue
2 sheets of typing paper
sheet of black or dark-colored construction paper
  (optional)
spiral-bound notebook or diary (at least 7 x 9 inches)

1. With pencil and ruler measure and mark a 6¼-by-1¼-inch-long strip on one sheet of construction paper. Measure and mark another strip of the same size on the second sheet of construction paper.

2. On the third sheet of construction paper, measure and mark a narrower, 6¼-by-1-inch strip.

3. Cut out the 3 strips. Glue the strips to the sheet of typing paper, with the narrow strip in the middle.

4. Draw four lines across the strips, 1¼ inches apart, as shown by the dashed lines.

5. Cut along the pencil lines, so that your 3 strips are now 5 smaller strips.

6. Place the strips on the second sheet of typing paper. Tip the strips at an angle as shown in the picture on page 95. Notice how the top and bottom of the middle strip line up all the way across.

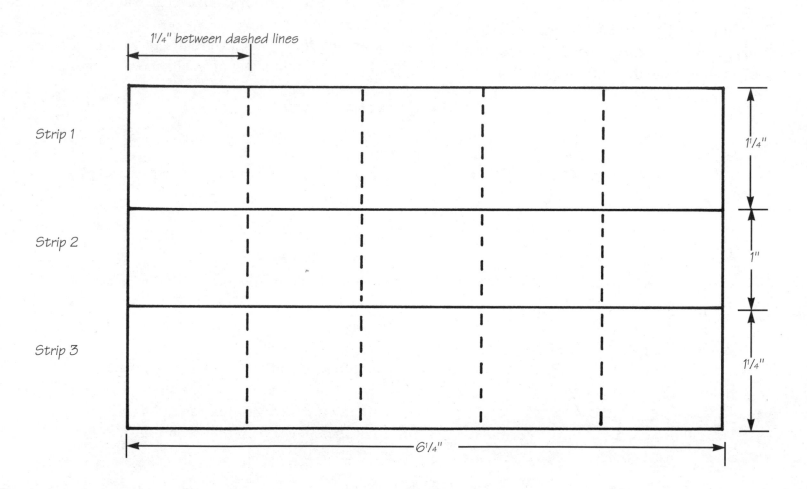

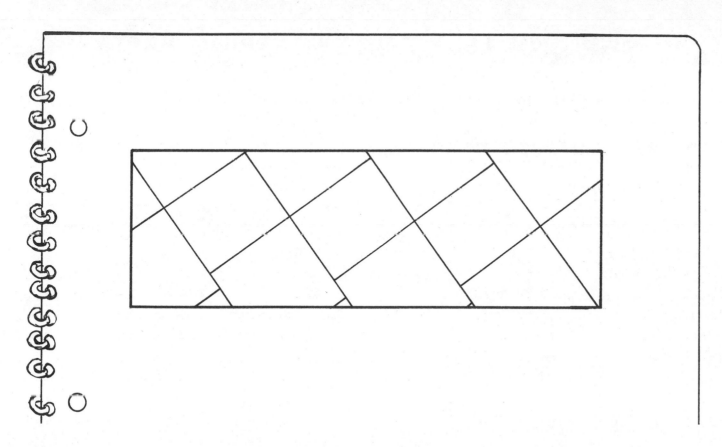

7. When you are pleased with how the strips are lined up, glue them to the typing paper.

8. With pencil and ruler, copy the dotted cutting lines shown in the picture. Plan the lines so that you'll cut off as little of the band as possible.

9. Cut out the patchwork band along the dotted lines. The completed band will be cut about 6¼ inches long and 2 inches high.

10. Place the patchwork band on the front cover of the book. Position it in the center and glue it to the cover. If you wish, you can cut two border strips out of the black or dark construction paper, ½ inch wide, to place at the top and bottom of the band.

11. Repeat these steps for the back cover if you want. Try to vary the pattern by making wider or narrower strips, for example, or by using different colors.

PROJECT — LEAF-PRINT WRAPPING PAPER

For leaf prints, fresh-picked leaves work best, but you can also use autumn leaves or pressed leaves that are not too dry. Leaves from houseplants can also be used—with permission, of course. The printed paper will have an attractive, natural look.

MATERIALS

several sheets of newspaper
white wrapping paper or heavy tissue paper
3 or 4 leaves in different shapes
medium paintbrush
acrylic paints or poster paints: your choice of 2 or 3
  colors
paper towels
rolling pin or wooden spoon

1. Spread newspaper over your work area. Place a sheet of wrapping paper on top.

2. Choose a leaf that is whole, with clear veins on the back. Brush a thin coat of paint on the back of the leaf, covering it completely.

3. Position the leaf on the wrapping paper, paint side down.

4. Fold a paper towel in half and place it over the leaf. Use a rolling pin to roll over the covered leaf. Make two or three firm rolling strokes, but don't press so hard that you crush the veins of the leaf.

5. Remove the paper towel and carefully lift the leaf off the paper. You should have a perfect impression of the leaf, with the veins standing out darker.

6. Repeat steps 2 through 5 with the same leaf, or use another. Make as many prints as you wish, positioning them in rows or in any pattern that looks pleasing to you.

Leaf print on paper

EVENING FUN

By the end of the holiday season, the shorter days of winter meant long, dark evenings. After supper, the family gathered around the fireplace. By the light of the fire and a few candles, they spent some evenings working on the projects. Mrs. Butler would weave, while Mr. Butler mended a piece of harness, Liz wrote in her diary, and Sam made a new fishing pole. On some evenings, they all worked together on the same project, like braided rugs.

Because the light from the fire and the candles was dim, the evening projects did not last long. Usually, everyone went to bed early, but sometimes they stayed up late. They sang songs and took turns reading aloud. They played games like tangram, checkers, or the beanbag target game.

Often they simply talked about the next farming season. They discussed the need to grow more wheat and the possibility of adding a room to the cabin for the dairy.

Sam liked to talk about the news that the first wagon trains had crossed the Great Plains and the Rocky Mountains to a place called Oregon. While Sam wondered what that journey would be like, the rest of the pioneer family felt that they were as far west as they wanted to go.

 **TANGRAM**

The Chinese puzzle game tangram looks quite easy. It is simply a square cut into seven shapes, called tans. But trying to arrange those seven shapes into a picture is a challenge. The player must arrange all seven tans (none can be left out) into the shape of a building, animal, chair, sailboat, pentagon, or some other object or shape. After you make your set of tans, have a contest with a friend to see who can make the most shapes.

MATERIALS

pencil
ruler
8-inch-square piece of cardboard or poster board
scissors

1. With pencil and ruler, mark three dots along the base and top of the poster board 2 inches apart as shown. Do the same on the sides.

2. Use the ruler to draw lines lightly in pencil to join the dots. You'll have a grid of sixteen 2-inch squares.

3. With pencil and ruler, mark the five bold cutting lines as shown. Mark these lines heavily so you will know where to cut.

4. Cut along the bold lines to form the 7 pieces called tans. Your tangram set is ready.

2" between grid lines, across and down

tan 2

tan 6

tan 1

tan 5

tan 4

tan 3

tan 7

Cut only on bold lines.

A Chinese Puzzle

According to Chinese legend, tangram was created by accident. A man was carrying a precious tile, but he dropped it and the tile broke into seven pieces. No matter how he arranged them, he could not get them back into a square shape.

Tangram was brought to the United States by the first immigrants from China in the early 1830s. Within ten years, the puzzle game swept the country and became one of the great fads of the 1800s. Contests were held to see who could design never-before-seen shapes. Tangram books and magazines offered dozens of new ideas. It is said that nearly 2,000 different tangram shapes are known.

5. To play tangram, you must use all 7 tans. Also, the pieces cannot overlap. Try making as many tangram shapes as you can think of. There are hundreds of possible tangram shapes. Here are some samples. How many others can you make?

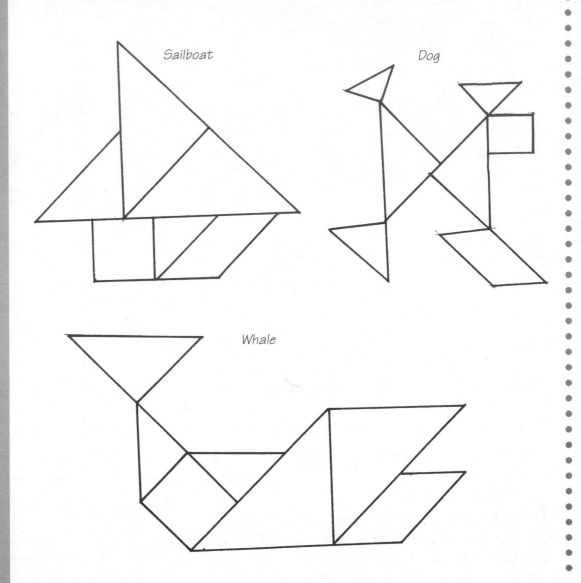

Sailboat

Dog

Whale

PROJECT FOLK ART CHECKERBOARD AND GAME

Pioneers made their own game boards for playing checkers, chess, and other games. They painted or stenciled pictures on the tray at either end of the board. (A stencil is a stiff sheet of material in which a design is cut so that paint applied on the sheet will reproduce the design on the surface underneath.) Some of the game boards were so beautifully made that people used them for wall decorations as well as for games.

You can make your own folk art checkerboard with a sun-and-moon design based on a game board of the 1800s. The dimensions have been scaled down to make a smaller board that is easy to store or carry, and just as easy to use. Pioneers made the checkers by cutting dried corncobs into disks, or by cutting an old broom handle. You can use clay for yours.

MATERIALS

several sheets of newspaper
8-by-12-inch piece of heavyweight poster board or
cardboard
ruler
pencil
red, black, yellow, light blue, and dark blue crayons or
markers
1-pound package of self-hardening clay
old table knife
red and black markers

1. Spread newspaper on your work surface. Place the poster board on it.

2. With ruler and pencil, make a line across both short ends of the board, 2 inches in from the ends. Measure carefully so that the lines are exactly 2 inches from the end all the way across. The center part of your board will now be a perfect 8-inch square. The 2-inch space at either end is called the tray, where you put your opponent's checkers when you capture them.

3. Use pencil and ruler to mark dots exactly 1 inch apart along all four sides as shown.

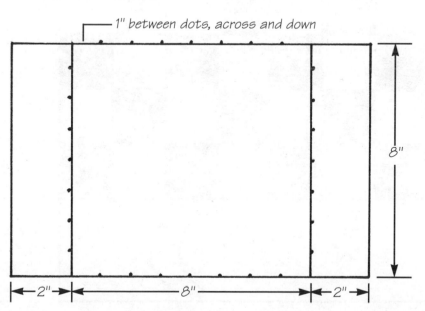
1" between dots, across and down

2" | 8" | 2"

8"

4. Carefully connect the dots with ruler and pencil. Your grid will have 64 perfect squares.

5. Color the squares red and black with the crayons, following the pattern as shown. (Dark squares are black; plain squares are red.)

6. Use the yellow crayon to draw the sun on one tray and the moon and star on the other. Color the background of the sun tray light blue and the background of the moon-and-star tray dark blue.

7. Remove the self-hardening clay from the package and knead it to make it soft. Roll about half the clay into a rope about 7 inches long and ³/₄ inch thick.

8. Use the table knife to cut the clay rope into 28 disks about ¼ inch thick. Let the clay dry according to the directions on the package.

9. Use markers to color 14 clay checkers red and 14 black. Twelve checkers are needed to play, so you'll have 2 extra in each color.

PROJECT BEANBAG TARGET GAME

American kids began playing with beanbags in the 1820s. They filled the bags with whatever was available, like dry beans, sand, or small pebbles. You can do the same to create your own target game to play indoors or out. The game is designed for two players, or two teams of two.

MATERIALS

2 old socks for each player or team
dry beans, gravel, or sand
scissors
string
2-foot-square piece of cardboard or poster board
marker or crayon
yardstick
1 or more players

1. Make each beanbag by filling an old sock with dry beans. Pack the stuffing tightly.

2. Tie a piece of string around the top of each sock. You may have to experiment a little to get the right amount of filler in each sock. You should be able to toss the beanbags with pretty good accuracy. If a beanbag seems lopsided, try tying the knot farther down from the top of the sock.

3. On the cardboard or poster board, use a marker to draw three circles as shown.

Rules for Checkers

1. Each player has 12 checkers. The checkers for both players move only on the black squares.

2. Each player lines up his or her checkers on the 12 black squares closest to his tray.

3. Black moves first. Each player must move one square at a time to the next black square. If the opponent's checker is in the way, the player jumps that checker, provided that the space she is jumping into is free. When a player jumps an opponent's checker, she captures it and places it in his tray.

4. Checkers can only move forward. But if a player gets a checker to his opponent's home line (the row closest to the opponent's tray), his checker is crowned and becomes a king. (Another checker is placed on top to identify it as a king.) Kings can move forward or backward, which gives them a great advantage.

5. The game ends when one player has lost all of his or her checkers, or is trapped and cannot make a move.

4. Write the numbers 1, 3, and 5 inside the circles as shown. These numbers indicate the number of points a player can score. If a beanbag lands on the outside circle, the player scores 1 point; if it lands on the next circle, she scores 3 points; and if it lands in the center circle, she scores 5 points. More than half the beanbag must be inside a circle to score points.

5. Use the yardstick to measure 10 feet from the cardboard target. Lay the yardstick down at the 10-foot mark. This will be your starting line.

6. Player 1 stands on the starting line and tosses 2 beanbags underhand. Don't count the scores yet.

7. Player 2 then tosses 2 bags, trying to score or to knock player 1's beanbags off the target.

8. After all 4 beanbags have been tossed, count the scores. If a beanbag lands on top of another, both scores count, as long as both are more than half inside a circle. Players take turns going first. The first player or team to reach 21 points wins.

GLOSSARY

Apache   A Native American tribe living in what is now the southwestern United States and northern Mexico.

bee   A social gathering for a specific purpose, such as quilting, husking corn, or peeling apples.

block   In patchwork sewing, a number of patches sewn together into a square design.

bowlers   A marbles game consisting of a square with a marble at each corner and one in the center, in which the object is to knock all five marbles out of the square.

chaff   The seed coverings and other waste that have to be separated from the seed in harvesting grains.

clowns   A group of male kachina dancers in the Southwestern tribes who entertain people during long religious ceremonies and poke fun at villagers who act like show-offs.

colonist   A person who settles in a new country.

cornmeal   Dried ground corn.

crock   A thick earthenware pot or jar.

daguerreotype   An early photograph invented by Frenchman Louis Daguerre in the 1830s.

dairy   A room or building where milk is kept and butter and cheese are made.

down   The soft, fluffy feathers of geese and other birds.

earthenware   A coarse form of pottery made by the pioneers and colonists.

flail   A wooden tool used in the harvesting of wheat to knock the kernels from the stalk.

fleece   The coat of wool sheared from sheep.

frontier   The area just beyond the settled regions of a country.

hogan   Navajo word for house.

homestead   A family's home and land.

Hopi   A Native American tribe living in what is now the state of Arizona.

Indian meal   The pioneer name for cornmeal.

jumping jack   A simple hand puppet, made of flat pieces of wood that can be made to dance or jump by pulling a string.

kachina   A male dancer who performs in the ceremonies of the Navajo and other Native American tribes of the Southwest; also the model of a kachina.

kiln   A special oven used to heat clay at high temperatures in order to harden it.

kilt   A skirtlike garment worn by the male kachina dancers of the Southwestern Native American tribes.

knuckling down   Shooting or pitching a marble with at least one knuckle resting on the ground.

lagging   Shooting marbles at a target line to decide which player goes first.

lasso   A long rope with a changeable noose used for roping cattle and horses on the frontier.

lean-to   A rough shed made of boards supported at one end by poles.

magic wallet   A toy made of two blocks of wood connected by ribbons, which seems to make a dollar bill magically move from one block to the other.

masa harina   Corn flour used in making tacos, burritos, enchiladas, and tortillas.

moshie   A game of marbles, also known as hundreds, in which each player shoots marbles at a hole called the pot.

Navajo   A large Native American tribe living in what is now New Mexico, Arizona, and southern Utah.

ojo de Dios   A yarn ornament created by Hispanic settlers in the Southwest used as a good-luck decoration during an October celebration.

pantin   French name for jumping jack.

patchwork   A method of sewing scraps of fabric together to make quilts and other items.

pictograph   A form of writing practiced by the Apache and other Native American tribes that uses pictures and symbols rather than words.

pioneer   A person who does something first; someone who first settles in an unsettled area.

plain weave   Two colors woven together to create a checkerboard pattern.

potter   A person who makes pottery.

pottery   Objects made by shaping clay, then hardening it.

ringer   A marbles game in which the target is a circle containing thirteen marbles that form a cross.

runners   A special group of kachina dancers in the Southwestern tribes who challenged the men and boys of the village to footraces.

salt glaze   The finish on some stoneware pottery created by throwing handfuls of salt into the kiln while the pots are being fired.

sandpainting   A type of ceremonial painting done with dry natural powders used by the Navajo and other Native American tribes.

Seminole   A Native American tribe that was originally part of the Creek nation but broke away in the 1700s to form a new tribe in southern Georgia and Florida.

Seminole patchwork   The method of sewing different color strips into bands to decorate clothing and other items.

shrub   A beverage made of fruit juice and sugar.

sickle   A farm tool with a sharp, curved blade used to cut grain or tall grass.

silhouette   A portrait cut from dark material and mounted on a light background.

singer   A specially trained Navajo who performs religious ceremonies that include making sandpaintings.

spongeware   A type of pottery from the 1800s decorated by paint applied with a sponge.

spoon bread   A puddinglike bread served as a warm side dish with meat or poultry.

stencil   A stiff sheet of material in which a design is cut so that paint applied on the sheet will reproduce the design on the surface underneath; also the painted design created by this method.

stoneware   Strong, heavy pottery.

switchel   A cold drink with a ginger flavor.

tan   One of the seven shapes cut from a square that are used in the Chinese puzzle game tangram.

tangram   A Chinese puzzle game made of a square divided into seven shapes, or tans, which are arranged to form figures.

thaumatrope   A simple toy that creates an optical illusion by spinning a disk with a different picture on each side.

thresh   To separate the seed from the rest of the grain by striking it with a flail or whip.

tray   The area at the end of a checkerboard where a player keeps checkers captured from an opponent.

weather vane   A movable object that turns on a pole to show wind direction.

whirligig   A toy with arms, wings, or paddles that whirl rapidly in the wind.

winnow   To remove the chaff from grain using a current of air.

Zuni   A Native American tribe living in what is now the state of New Mexico.

BIBLIOGRAPHY

Suzanne I. Barchers & Patricia C. Marden. *Cooking Up U.S. History: Recipes and Research to Share with Children.* Chicago: Teachers Ideas Press, 1991.

Cobblestone, The History Magazine for Young People. 30 Grove Street, Peterborough, NH, 03458
> *The Oregon Trail,* Dec. 1981
> *Old Sturbridge Village,* Feb. 1982
> *Children's Toys,* Dec. 1986
> *America's Folk Art,* Aug. 1991

Cheryl Edwards, Ed. *Westward Expansion: Exploration and Settlement.* Carlisle, MA: Discovery Enterprises, 1992.

Katharine N. Emsden, Ed. *Voices From the West: Life Along the Trail.* Carlisle, MA: Discovery Enterprises, 1992.

Leonard Everett Fisher. *The Oregon Trail.* New York: Holiday House, 1990.

Barbara Greenwood. *A Pioneer Sampler: The Daily Life of a Pioneer Family in 1840.* New York: Ticknor & Fields, 1995.

Lynda Hatch. *The Santa Fe Trail.* New York: Good Apple, 1994.

Joanne Landers Henry. *A Clearing in the Forest: A Story About a Real Settler Boy.* New York: Four Winds, 1992.

David C. King. *America's Story, Book 4: The Westward Movement, 1770s-1850s.* Littleton, MA: Sundance, 1996.

Jean Lipman & Alice Winchester. *The Flowering of American Folk Art, 1776-1876.* Philadelphia: Running Press, 1987.

Martin W. Sandler. *Pioneers, A Library of Congress Book.* New York: HarperCollins, 1994.

Eric Sloane. *Diary of an Early American Boy.* New York: Random House, 1965.

Marlene Smith-Baranzini and Howard Egger-Bovet. *Book of the New American Nation.* Brown Paper School U.S. Kids History. Boston: Little, Brown, 1995.

Evelyn Toynton. *Growing Up in America: 1830-1860.* Brookfield, CT: Millbrook Press, 1995.

Laura Ingalls Wilder. *Little House In the Big Woods.* New York: Harper & Row, 1932; *Little House on the Prairie,* 1935; *Farmer Boy,* 1933.

INDEX

A

African trade beads, 39
air-dried flowers, 10
Apache scroll, 51
apple butter, 59

B

beanbag target game, 103

C

Canadian goose whirligig, 78
checkers, 103
Chinese puzzle, 100
Christmas tree, 85
compass, 17
cornhusk doll, 66
cornmeal, 15
cricket thermometer, 19

D

Daguerre, Louis, 90

E

earthenware, 6
Erie canal, 62

F

finding direction, 17
folk art checkerboard, 101
frontier medicine, 75

H

Halloween ghosts, 69
hasty pudding, 13
hay-time switchel, 33
Hopi kachina doll, 49
Howe, Elias, 25

I

ice, 35

J

johnnycakes, 14
jumping jack, 27

K

kachina, 49
knots, 20

L

leaf-print wrapping paper, 96
lemonade, 34

M

magic wallet, 74

marbles, 45

masa harina, 71

medicine, 75

moving toys, 77

N

Navajo sandpainting, 54

O

ojo de Dios, 87

old-time lemonade, 43

P

patchwork picture, 22

picture frame, 92

pinecone angel, 83

Polaris (North Star), 18

portraits, 90

Q

quilting bee, 22

R

roasted pumpkin seeds, 63

S

salt dough ornaments, 84

sandpainting, 56

Seminole patchwork, 93

sewing machine, 25

silhouette portrait, 90

Singer, Isaac M., 25

soda pop, 36

spongeware clay pot, 7

spoon bread, 61

stencil, 101

stoneware, 9

strawberry shrub, 35

sweet grass, 42

T

tangram, 99

Thanksgiving, 82

thaumatrope, 30

tortillas, 71

Tudor, Frederic, 35

tying knots, 20

W

whirligig, 78

woodchoppers, 76

woven mat, 41

Wyeth, Nathaniel, 35